COLLECTING

ORIGINAL

CARTOON ART

Bob Bennett

Cover Design: Ann Eastburn
Interior Layout: Anthony Jacobson

Library of Congress Catalog
Card Number 87-50018

ISBN 0-87069-486-3

10   9   8   7   6   5   4   3   2   1

Published by

Wallace-Homestead Book Company
580 Waters Edge
Lombard, Illinois 60148

One of the
ABC PUBLISHING
Companies

Contents

Acknowledgments

My thanks to the following people for graciously donating items from their collections: Sig Armitage, Bob Beehm, Fred Bennetto, Jr., Judy Ann Burton, Bridget Cacace, Norman Bruce Caldwell, Phyllis Goldman, Paul Hartunian, Jeanne Hoyt, Eugene Kirschenbaum, Newton Lane, Robert A. LeGresley, Maree Lubran, Greg Lundy, Sherri McKnight, Larry Marshall, Eric Niderost, Jeff Nobel, Ronald Raposa, Bob Rubin, Al Showalterbough, Ray Ward, Bob Weaver, Jim Weaver, and Bart Wilson.

I am especially grateful to the many artists and illustrators who contributed to the success of this project by providing original artwork, permission to use examples of their work, and many interesting and informative anecdotes.

Specifically, the following deserve recognition: Ron Barrett, Ernie Chan, Jack Elrod, Friz Freleng, Ferd Johnson, Bil Keane, Hank Ketcham, Walter Lantz, Dr. Seuss, and Virginia and George Smith.

The noted autograph author, Charles Hamilton, deserves credit for generously allowing me to use many of his fine illustrations of comic and illustration art, as well as many celebrity self-portraits.

I thank my father, Robert W. Bennett, for assistance in photographing items from my collection for this book, and my gratitude to Bene, Steve Costello, Pat Reardon, Michele Schwartz, and Brian ("computers are his forte") Rapalje for their suggestions and support.

Introduction

It is difficult to overestimate the importance of the cartoon as a popular art form. Cartoons are scattered throughout countless books, magazines, and newspapers, and abound in the movies and on television. Political and social statements are often communicated more effectively through the medium of the cartoon. Famous character creations have become merchandising symbols for hundreds of diverse products, and some have even become symbols of popular culture. Although the popularity of the cartoon can be traced back almost one hundred years, it is only recently that we have seen tremendous increases in the critical appreciation and influence of cartoons.

In the last decade, critical reaction to animated movie and television cartoons has changed drastically. For years, only Walt Disney films attracted critical attention, but today many animated shorts of the forties and fifties are perceived as classic films, and their animators recognized as masters of cinematic technique. Even some early television cartoons have a newfound popularity, largely due to their great appeal to members of the baby-boom generation.

One of B. Kliban's famous sketches of a cat, **$15.**

The comic strip has recently ventured beyond the newspaper into the realm of best selling books. It is not surprising to look at a list of current bestsellers and find that three or four are collections of popular strips, usually "Garfield," "Doonesbury," or "The Far Side." In addition, the comic strip is changing dramatically. Controversial subjects and more adult humor have found a wider and more diverse audience, and this new approach is starting to prevail over one-shot gags and adventure stories, hallmarks of the comic form since its inception.

Editorial and political cartoonists have always enjoyed respect and a younger generation of artists, armed with satire and a sharp wit, are carrying forward this tradition.

As might be imagined, the growing popularity of cartoons has led to an explosion in memorabilia related to animation and to the cartoon in all its various forms. But while many collectors of this type of memorabilia are interested in comic books, films, clothing, and toys, relatively few have been interested in owning the original art itself. The collectors of original cartoon art instead consider themselves art collectors, akin to those who purchase the works of Rembrandt, Cezanne, and Picasso.

Some collectors of cartoon art engage in comparing the great masters to certain cartoonists. Sometimes these comparisons are not completely without merit, but are usually made so enthusiastically that it is difficult to take them seriously. A lively, easily stretched imagination is necessary if you're going to start looking for similarities in the works of Leonardo da Vinci and Walt Disney. It is possible, however, to make less extravagant

Original drawing by *The New Yorker* cartoonist Charles Addams, **$10.**

comparisons between cartoons and fine art. Like great works of art, certain comic strips and animated films have exhibited a high degree of specialized artistic skill. And a great many cartoons, including the political drawings of Thomas Nast and Jules Feiffer, as well as many of the early comic strips, did not lack serious literary or intellectual value.

There are also some interesting differences between comic and fine art. Many works by the great masters were commissioned by European royalty, and often served to reinforce the social structures of the period. In contrast, the cartoon arose to parody royalty and the upper classes in the form of caricatures. Early caricaturists, like Goya and Daumier, used their drawings to express extreme hostility to eighteenth century Spanish and French monarchies.

This contrast between fine art and comic art is also interesting in regard to collecting and owning original artwork. A work of fine art is unique; there is only one original, and only one person can own and enjoy it (unless of course it is owned by a museum open to the public). But consider the fact that thousands of drawings, produced by the same group of people, are used in the making of an animated cartoon; thousands can own original drawings of Donald Duck, Mickey Mouse, or Bugs Bunny. Comic strip artists produce a signed, original panel for publication every single day, and, if these are not readily available, the cartoonist, his assistants, or successors, might be persuaded to create more originals. This is not to say that there are no unique or rare items of cartoon art available for purchase. It is only to suggest that cartoon art may be owned

Edward Koren, original drawing, $10.

Ronald Reagan, by editorial cartoonist Eldon Pletcher, $15.

7

W.B. Park, $10.

Frank Kelly Freas, $5.

Political cartoonist Dick Locher, self-portrait, $5.

by vastly greater numbers of people than fine art. Cartoon art is a popular art form in the truest sense. It is accessible to virtually everyone.

Collecting cartoon art, whether a hobby or something more significant, has not yet become as popular in America as it is in Europe. Many Europeans idolize famous cartoonists and animators, and original cartoon art hangs in museums as renowned as the Louvre. In America, collecting illustration art, which we will cover in chapter 5, has been popular for several years, but the art of the comic strip and the animated film is only beginning to attract collectors. Since Americans have often followed European trends in fashion, music, film, and fine art, it will be no surprise if cartoon art becomes as collectible here, especially since comic strips and movie cartoons are uniquely American.

Already, there are signs that cartoon art collecting will reach a tremendous level of popularity in America. A growing body of expensive and magnificently produced books featuring original cartoon art in the tradition of books on fine art, such as the work of Van Gogh or Raphael, mirror the

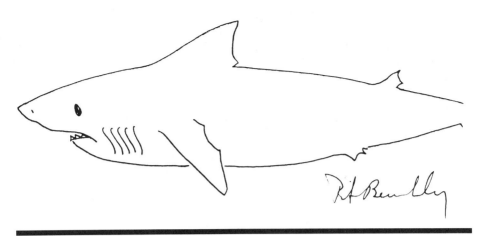

Original drawing of a shark by the author of *Jaws*, Peter Benchley, **$20.**

trend. Two fairly recent books are *The Illusion of Life* (Abbeville Press: 1984) dealing with the Walt Disney films, and *Tex Avery* (1986) by Patrick Brion, a massive work about the greatest comic genius of the animated cartoon.

Recent prices paid ·for original cartoon art are also a sure sign of its growing popularity. The average original daily strip sells for $75 to $100, but much higher prices have been paid for rare strips or those that are highly sought. An original strip by the distinguished early cartoonist Lyonel Feininger recently sold for over $6,000. Drawings, sketches, or paintings by famous comic strip artists can also be worth a great deal, as evidenced by the recent sale for over $15,000 of a color painting of "The Yellow Kid" by R.F. Outcault. Rare animation drawings continually bring high prices as well. Film director Steven Spielberg paid over $18,000 for an animation cel (a drawing on celluloid used in the making of a film) of Peter Pan and Tinkerbell from the Walt Disney classic.

Prestigious auction houses now list hundreds of pieces of cartoon art in their catalogs, and firms such as Christie's and Guernsey's have gone so

Original drawing of Chico Marx by his brother Harpo, **$200.**

Paul Szep, Pulitzer prize-winning editorial cartoonist for *The Boston Globe,* self-portrait, $10.

far as to feature auctions limited exclusively to animation or comic art. Even a museum of cartoon art in Rye Brook, New York, has been founded by the creator of the strip "Beetle Bailey," Mort Walker. These developments are strong evidence that cartoon art is gradually being recognized as a serious branch of art.

As a hobby, collecting cartoon art has not advanced very rapidly. There are no clubs or organizations devoted to collecting cartoon art, and no publications dealing exclusively with the subject. Most hobbyists, as opposed to serious art collectors who are interested in cartoon art, are autograph, film, or comic collectors who dabble in collecting original cartoons.

Finding material to collect can also be somewhat difficult. You will find that most animation artwork is owned by the studios and is rarely released to the public. However, studio policy of retaining original art is relatively recent; in the 1940s and 1950s some studios discarded this material, apparently unaware of its potential value. The Disney studios have maintained the most complete files of animation

"How Come You Know So Much About Sin?" Original cartoon by Jeffrey J. Monahan, **$20.**

material, but this is only one reason why Disney art carries great value since it is in very high demand.

Another problem in finding material is generated by the fact that many animators and cartoonists are collectors themselves. They often are reluctant to part with their own strips or drawings, and sometimes they are avid purchasers of the work of fellow artists. Nevertheless, many cartoonists and animators are very generous in sharing their strips or making original drawings for collectors. A few cartoonists sell their work, and sometimes a good bargain can be found in this manner.

Despite the problems, collecting cartoon art is a very rewarding endeavor. A great deal can be learned about the comics, movie cartoons, and even art in general, that is also tremendously useful in building your collection. In collecting cartoon art you will gain an insight into the processes involved in making a comic strip or an animated cartoon, and may even have the opportunity to get in touch with your favorite cartoonist or animator. More importantly, you can have a great deal of fun. If you enjoy cartoons, you will certainly enjoy collecting the artwork itself.

Mel Yauk, **$5.**

Walt Disney animator and *The New Yorker* cartoonist Eldon Dedini, **$10.**

Original cartoon art makes attractive and exciting displays at a reasonable price. You may never hang a Rembrandt in your living room, but what about an original drawing of Mickey Mouse by Walt Disney? If you are lucky enough to find one of these (you'll find out why they are probably more scarce than a Rembrandt in chapter 2), you will own an item with cultural and historical value that the average person will recognize and appreciate. Because cartoon art is colorful, humorous, and often of very high artistic quality, it is a wonderful collectible for display purposes.

Cartoon art is still relatively inexpensive, because it is only beginning to be widely collected in this country. It is almost sure to become amazingly popular, but many bargains can be had at the present time. Original art at inexpensive prices can be a good investment, particularly if it has cultural or artistic significance. Cartoon art possesses both characteristics.

Morrie Turner, original drawing of characters from his strip "Wee Pals," **$25.** By permission of News America Syndicate.

Cartoon art is presently a very good investment, but there are dangers to be aware of, as when investing in any collectible. Once interest in a collectible spurts, speculators and investors will enter the picture, and their activities push prices to unrealistically high levels. When this happens, the speculative "bubble" may burst, causing a drastic decline in prices. .

Besides the activities of speculators, you should be aware of changes in the economy that might give investors the wrong signal for the proper time to buy and sell. In a period of high inflation, investing too heavily should be avoided, as eventually the inflationary period will end and prices will fall.

A few simple guidelines should be followed to avoid making poor investments. First, seek quality above all else. Purchase the works of the most respected cartoonists or animators, not the unknown or neglected. Interesting, rare, or unique items are also wise choices for investment purposes. Second, the best investments in cartoon art are those items that are most easily liquidated, i.e., those easy to sell to others. Items having a high unit value are preferable, since if you have to sell quickly, it is best to have to sell only a few items, rather than hundreds. And, when keeping an eye on the economy, remember to buy during or after a recessionary situation, not before it.

Collecting cartoon art is becoming amazingly popular. Throughout this book, you'll be exposed to all of the areas of the hobby, from animation art to celebrity self-portraits. You'll learn what makes cartoon art valuable and be shown how to buy, sell, and obtain cartoon art on your own. In addition, histories of the comics, animation, and the editorial cartoon will be presented, so that it may be possible to appreciate not only the investment potential of the hobby, but also become aware of the important role the cartoon played and is playing in our culture.

1 Collecting Cartoon Art

Once you decide to start a collection, you need to determine what kind of material you want to collect and then learn where and how to obtain it. In this chapter, we will examine ways to approach the hobby and offer tips on building and improving your collection.

Those who are interested in collecting cartoon art for investment purposes should understand why certain cartoon art can have great monetary value, and how that value is determined. As with all commodities, the price of cartoon art is determined by supply and demand. Supply refers to the scarcity of the item, while demand measures the intensity of consumer preference. Like most collectibles, demand is the more important factor in assessing the value of cartoon art, since if no one wants a certain collectible, it really doesn't matter how scarce it is. Scarcity is important only to the extent that if an item is in great demand, its rarity will serve to further increase the price.

Supply and demand are the most important measures of value, and the other factors will follow logically. As with any collectible, condition can be extremely important in determining the price of cartoon art. This makes sense because collectors prefer items in the best possible condition.

Magazine cartoonist Thomas Cheney, **$10.**

15

Sketch of a cat by the creator of the comic character Gordo, Gus Arriola, **$10.**

However, a very scarce item in great demand may carry a high price tag regardless of condition because collectors will consider themselves lucky to find the item at all.

The importance or significance of the item, either historically, culturally, or as a work of art will affect value. Critical appreciation may often bring about a high price, but remember that consumer valuations, not criticism, determines value. In deciding whether an item has historical or artistic significance, several criteria should be employed. The artist of the work and whether the character is immediately recognizable are of extreme importance. A signed sketch of Mickey Mouse by Walt Disney would carry a much greater value than one signed by Ub Iwerks, a Disney animator (even though Iwerks actually created Mickey). Similarly, an animation cel of Mickey Mouse is worth far more than one of a more obscure character, such as Chilly Willy or Hector Heathcote. The simple reason for this is the fact that buyers of cartoon art look for the most famous characters drawn by the most famous cartoonists and animators.

Also of importance is the role of a certain piece of cartoon art in a productive process (e.g., a "cel" in the making of an animated cartoon). Aside from its artistic value, cartoon art that is essential or important in making an animated cartoon or strip, can have tremendous value. The material used in an animated film includes cels on which the characters are inked, as well as storyboards, preliminary drawings, and backgrounds. Storyboards and preliminary drawings are usually worth the most since they are fewer in number, but an especially famous scene inked on a cel or group of cels may carry a greater price. Drawings on cels are usually more refined and colorful, which also increases their value. In cartoon strips, the original strip is almost always worth more than a sketch of a character by the cartoonist. The exception to this would be a particularly elaborate drawing or painting of a character.

BEST WISHES FROM
BRAD ANDERSON

Marmaduke creator Brad Anderson has drawn several dogs, but not his famous character, **$20.**

Artistic significance is also shaped by the elaboration of a strip, animation drawing, or sketch. A quick sketch received from a cartoonist in person has considerably less value than a drawing that took an hour to complete. The cartoon strips that are worth the most are generally those that show greater artistic skill and dexterity, all other things being equal (i.e., fame of the artist or character). Some of the most valuable strips are those from cartoonists who were remarkably gifted artists, such as Winsor McCay, Lyonel Feininger, and Harold Foster. In addition to artistic skill, other things, such as whether the drawing was made in pencil or in color and the size of the drawing, can also affect price.

If you are interested in collecting illustration art for investment purposes, remember that in addition to the material we have covered, illustration art is more valuable if the illustrations are part of classic books. Originals by E. W. Kemble, the illustrator of

Huckleberry Finn, for example, show tremendous skill, but they are of value primarily because of the work in which they appeared. In general, illustration art is often a very good investment since the quality of the illustrations often approaches the level of fine art.

There also are good investments to be made in celebrity self-portraits, which are covered in chapter 6. These are more often found at autograph auctions and in autograph dealers' catalogs than at cartoon art sales. You should familiarize yourself with the autograph collecting market in order to pursue this material. Even within the autograph hobby, celebrity self-portraits are fairly hard to locate and they are unavailable for many celebrities who have refused to make them. When they can be found, values are determined by the celebrity's fame, as well as scarcity, and the elaboration of the drawing. Since the artists of these drawings are usually people of more

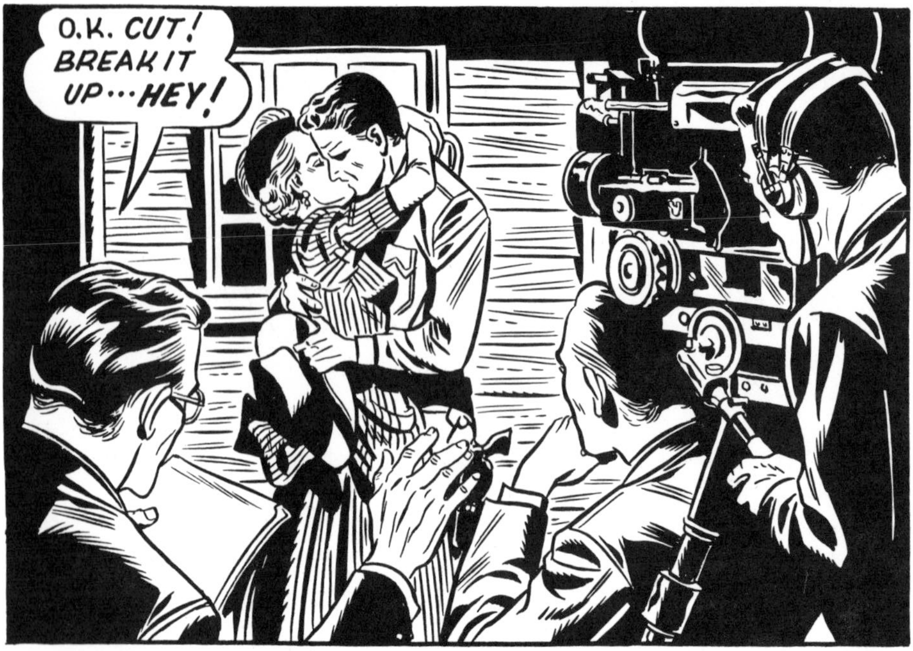
O.K. CUT! BREAK IT UP...HEY!

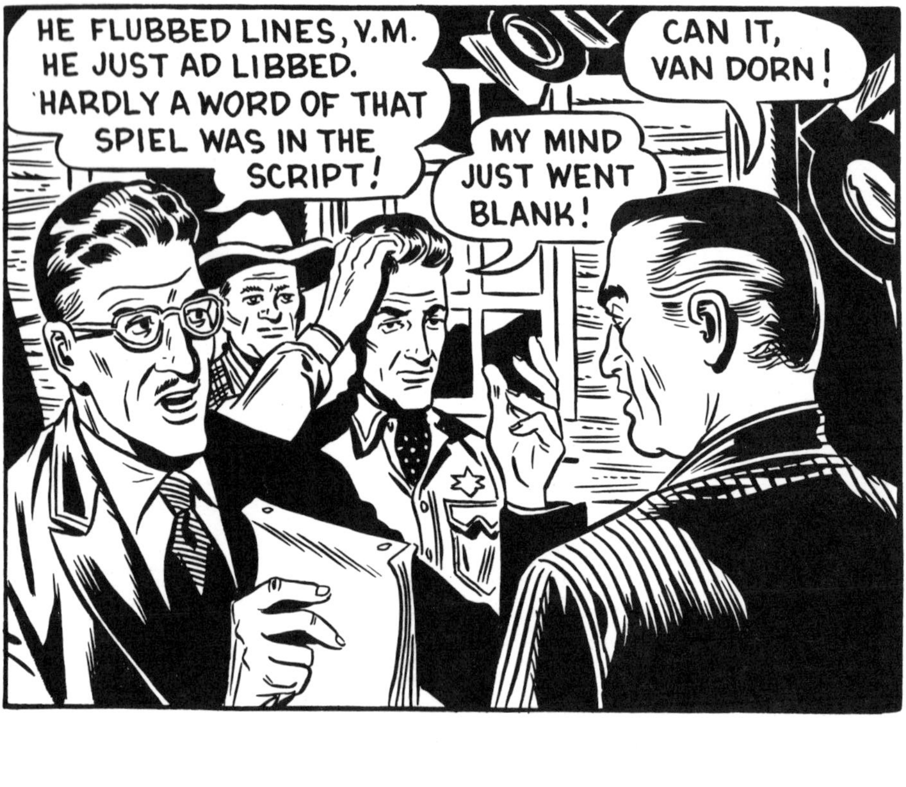
HE FLUBBED LINES, V.M. HE JUST AD LIBBED. 'HARDLY A WORD OF THAT SPIEL WAS IN THE SCRIPT!
MY MIND JUST WENT BLANK!
CAN IT, VAN DORN!

Original Australian comic strip "Smoky Dawson," by Albert DeVine, $50.

you won't assemble an in-depth collection in a specific area. Second, you will probably end up with the most readily available material in each area, with the result that your collection will lack exclusiveness. This is fine, of course, and can be interesting. If you wish to limit your initial investment, you might try to obtain material that does not have high investment value, but is instead scarce or of great sentimental value.

renown than cartoonists, celebrity self-portraits can be priced higher than original cartoon sketches, although original strips and animation art average a higher price.

In deciding what area of cartoon art to collect from an investment standpoint, it is best to choose areas you already know or are interested in learning about. It is important to specialize because such a collection is easier to sell should you decide to liquidate. Another reason is that the value of your collection as a whole increases. If you have some relatively unimportant pieces in your collection, but your collection is focused on one area, you may still receive more for the entire collection than you would selling individual pieces. Collecting at random from different areas may be enjoyable to you, but if you are concerned about investment, this approach has two major flaws. First,

John Lane, $10.

Dick Moores, **$20.**

Specialization is a good idea, even when investment value and potential is of no real concern. Because you may not have time to research and learn about all the areas of cartoon art collecting, it may be best to concentrate in the area most appealing to you. This technique will enable you to improve the quality of your collection tremendously. If your collecting energy is expended into one or two small, manageable areas, you should be able to find rarer and more desirable material, and you will emerge with a thorough knowledge of a given field.

Peter Arno, **$15.**

Walter Lantz, the creator of Woody Woodpecker, and his wife Gracie who supplied the voice, signed photograph, **$15.** ©1986 Walter Lantz Productions, Inc.

Rudolph Wendelin, original drawing of Smokey the Bear, **$40.**

Bugs Bunny by Chuck Jones, **$20.** ©Warner Brothers, Inc.

Once you have decided which material you would like to obtain, your next problem is acquisition. Certain types of cartoon art are difficult to locate at various times, and there are few people who consistently deal in all material. If you decide to collect original comic strips or signed sketches of comic strip artists, you can find many sellers by reading publications devoted to the comics or comic collecting. Most of the advertisements in such publications will pertain to comic books or comic sections from old newspapers, but a few people advertise original art. One of the best of these publications is *Comics Buyer's Guide,* which has a fairly large readership. In addition to providing advertisements from sellers, the publication also lists comic conventions—excellent places to see and buy original art. Another useful publication is *Paper Collectors' Marketplace.* This is primarily an advertising publication, but it

"IT'S BEEN THREE HOURS — HOW LONG DOES IT TAKE THE GABOOZLE TO WARM UP?"

Roy Cruse, original cartoon, **$15.**

can put you in touch with many dealers and is worth receiving. Advertising rates are inexpensive, so consider placing want ads requesting the material you are interested in purchasing. The highest quality comic art, as well as animation and illustration material, is often listed for sale by dealers or auction in the "Arts & Leisure" section of the Sunday *New York Times.* Both *Comics Buyer's Guide* and *Paper Collectors' Marketplace* list many upcoming auctions, and auction reports and announcements can also be found in journals devoted to antiques and paper collectibles.

Fleischer Studios animator, Leslie Carbarga, **$25.**

Animation art sellers can be located in many of the above publications, although comic art predominates in both *Comics Buyer's Guide* and *Paper Collectors' Marketplace*. Animation art can also be found in several papers dealing with the collecting of movie memorabilia. A few publications that carry these advertisements include *American Film, Movie Collector's World, The Big Reel,* and *Classic Images.*

Original sketches made by cartoonists expressly for collectors are usually sold by dealers specializing in autographs. Celebrity self-portraits are sold by autograph dealers. There are only a handful of autograph collectors who pursue this type of material, but dealers of such usually charge reasonable prices, and examples from many different cartoonists are available. A list of autograph dealers who sell original sketches is provided in the Appendix.

Quality illustration art is available mainly at auction, but a few private sellers occasionally place their advertisements in antiques, paper collectibles, or art journals. However, material that is not of tremendous value or significance is often available from autograph dealers, book dealers, and sellers of animation or comic art.

The greatest difficulty you will experience in buying original art from a dealer is deciding the proper price to pay. Most other difficulties are minor, and once you become familiar with prices, you should encounter few problems. Collecting cartoon art is a lot less tricky than collecting fine art, autographs, or many other collectibles

where the authenticity of an item is crucial. Forgeries of cartoon art are still rare. As the hobby grows in popularity they will likely become more prevalent, especially since the forgery of a cartoon character is much simpler than the forgery of a painting. We will examine the issue of authenticity later in this chapter. It can pose a problem for the inexperienced buyer and seller, alike.

Although the prices listed in this book should be of assistance to you in determining the proper prices to pay for cartoon art, there are other steps you should take as well. If you are in search of rarer or more valuable material, we recommend that you read the auction reports for cartoon art that are provided in antiques and paper collectibles magazines or art journals. In many cases these reports provide a little background information about the auction itself, making it easier to determine if the prices realized were justified or unrealistic. If you are buying less expensive material, solicit price listings from as many sellers as possible. Write to sellers who advertise in the publications you receive to get some idea of the average price for the kind of material you are looking for. Examine lists for several months so that you can acquaint yourself with prices and with the various sellers before buying. Of course, if you come across especially rare material, or something you simply must have in your collection, you should purchase it as long as you exercise reasonable caution.

Besides pricing, there are other matters of importance to remember in selecting which seller to patronize. A good description of the condition of the item from the seller is vital. You do not want to purchase an item thinking that it is in excellent condition only to find that it is torn, stained, or very faded. A good description not only provides accurate information concerning condition, but also informs you as to whether the drawing is in pencil or in color, and the size and elaboration of the artwork. The seller should also furnish a clearly understood statement of his return policy, and this return provision should cover any area of dissatisfaction with the material.

Buying from dealers can be somewhat difficult at times, but usually the primary difficulty is in finding a seller with the items you have chosen to collect. Most private sellers of cartoon art are relatively inexpensive sources, at least when compared to buying at auction. Once you begin collecting cartoon art, you will find that there are auctions where prices are similar to those charged by sellers of cartoon art, but that there are also extremely expensive auctions. The latter usually feature premier material, but if you watch dealer advertising, you can also purchase high-quality items from them.

Cartoon art auctions are similar to auctions of fine art, especially since the successful bidders are generally very wealthy individuals. Unless you have a great deal of money to spend on cartoon art, and time to travel (since these auctions rarely allow for bidding by mail), you will likely have to forego them as a source of material. Announcements are provided in art and

RUBE GOLDBERG

Dear Mr. Palmer:

I have your letter inviting me to participate in the cartoon show you are planning for the bank. Tom mentioned this when he was down here over the Fourth.

When I go into town I'll dig up a few originals and send them along to you before July 28th, your deadline. The art show was really beautiful and I hope the cartoon exhibition will approach its high standard, if not in beauty, then in interest.

Thanks for asking me to join your distinguished group. I feel flattered.

sincerely

Rube Goldberg

Letter signed by Rube Goldberg, famous for the "Rube Goldberg contraptions," $25.

National Lampoon cartoonist Sharry Flenniken, $10.

antiques publications and, if the opportunity presents itself, by all means attend one for the educational benefit and enjoyment of it.

Auctions of lesser importance than those mentioned above are often announced in the same publications where you find sellers of cartoon art. Auctions are also advertised or mentioned in Arts or Living sections of major newspapers. The *New York Times* Sunday "Arts & Leisure" section regularly features these advertisements. Furthermore, in addition to being less expensive, many of these auctions will accept bids by mail. When bidding at auction, it is best to have a working knowledge of prices. Some auctions feature minimum bid levels that can be a helpful guide, but this information should be treated with caution, since the minimum prices may be set at unreasonably high levels. As with purchasing from a seller, try to acquaint yourself with the prices of material you are interested in before proceeding. This should not be difficult for you if you take the time to solicit as many listings and catalogs as are available.

If you wish to trade or sell items from your collection, your best bet is to advertise in the same publications where you have seen cartoon art advertised. Comic art is best sold through comic publications and paper collectible magazines, while animation art is usually more easily sold to people who read film publications like *Classic Images* or *American Film*. Illustration art should be advertised for sale

TO—
RAYMOND
WARD

WITH ALL GOOD WISHES
FROM THE BUMSTEADS

and CHIC
YOUNG
2/27/73

Printed sketch of the Bumsteads, authentically signed by Chic Young, **$35.** Reprinted with special permission of King Features Syndicate, Inc.

in antiques and paper collectible journals, while celebrity self-portraits, tied as they are to autograph collecting, can more easily be sold to autograph dealers or through autograph publications.

Again, knowledge of pricing is essential in selling or trading your material. You want to get the most for your material either in cash or in trade, and if you are not familiar with prices, you may find yourself on the losing end of these transactions. If you are not completely familiar with current prices, but still need to sell your collection, advertise it for a slightly higher price than you believe is reasonable. The market will inform you whether your price is too high or low. People will either shy away from purchasing your material, or else you will be besieged with prospective buyers.

Also important in selling or trading is placing an effective advertisement. The cost of either classified or display advertising probably will figure in your decision, but there are other considerations as well. You should decide whether it is more effective to place a classified ad stating that you have a list of material available for sale or trade, or to place a display ad listing precisely what you have for sale. This is an important decision, because sometimes a good, in-depth description is necessary to explain why the item is worth the price you are asking. In the display ad you may only be able to list a Bugs Bunny animation drawing for sale. Prices for a Bugs Bunny cel usually start at $100 or so, but your cel is from 1937 and was used in the first Bugs Bunny cartoon (where Bugs

Milton Caniff, Charles M. Schulz, Roy Crane, Jim Davis

made only a brief appearance). This information justifies your higher-than-normal asking price. A well-written ad giving condition or the significance of the item and other distinquishing characteristics is usually more effective when rare material is offered for sale. Of course, when you decide to advertise, you will also have to consider how much material you wish to sell and how much space you will need in a display ad. The cost of the ad compared to the profit realized from the sale of your material is also important.

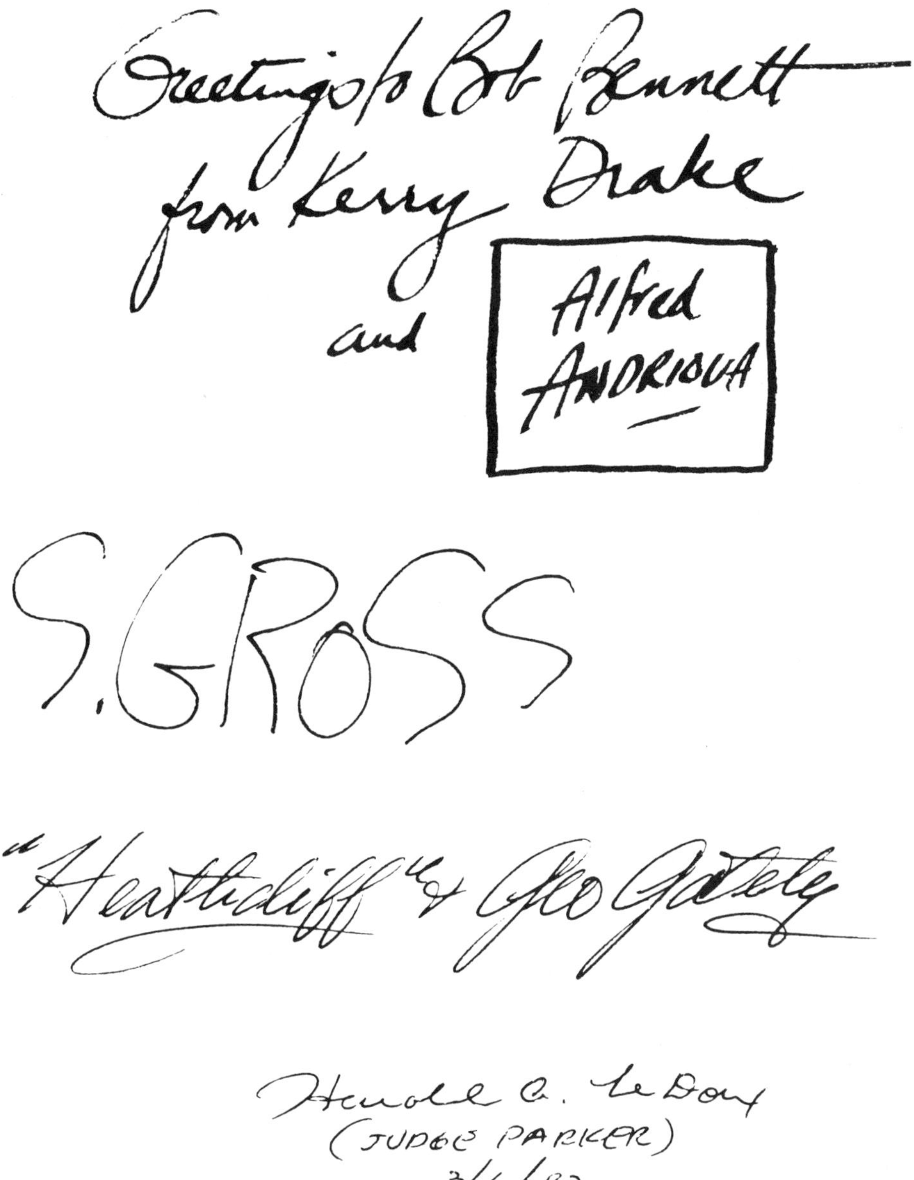

Greetings to Bob Bennett from Kerry Drake and *Alfred ANDRIOLA*

S. GROSS

"Heathcliff" & Geo Gately

Harold A. LeDoux
(JUDGE PARKER)
3/6/82

Alfred Andriola, Sam Gross, George Gately, Harold LeDoux.

Sy Barry, Mike Peters, Scrawls, Jules Feiffer, Al Hirschfield.

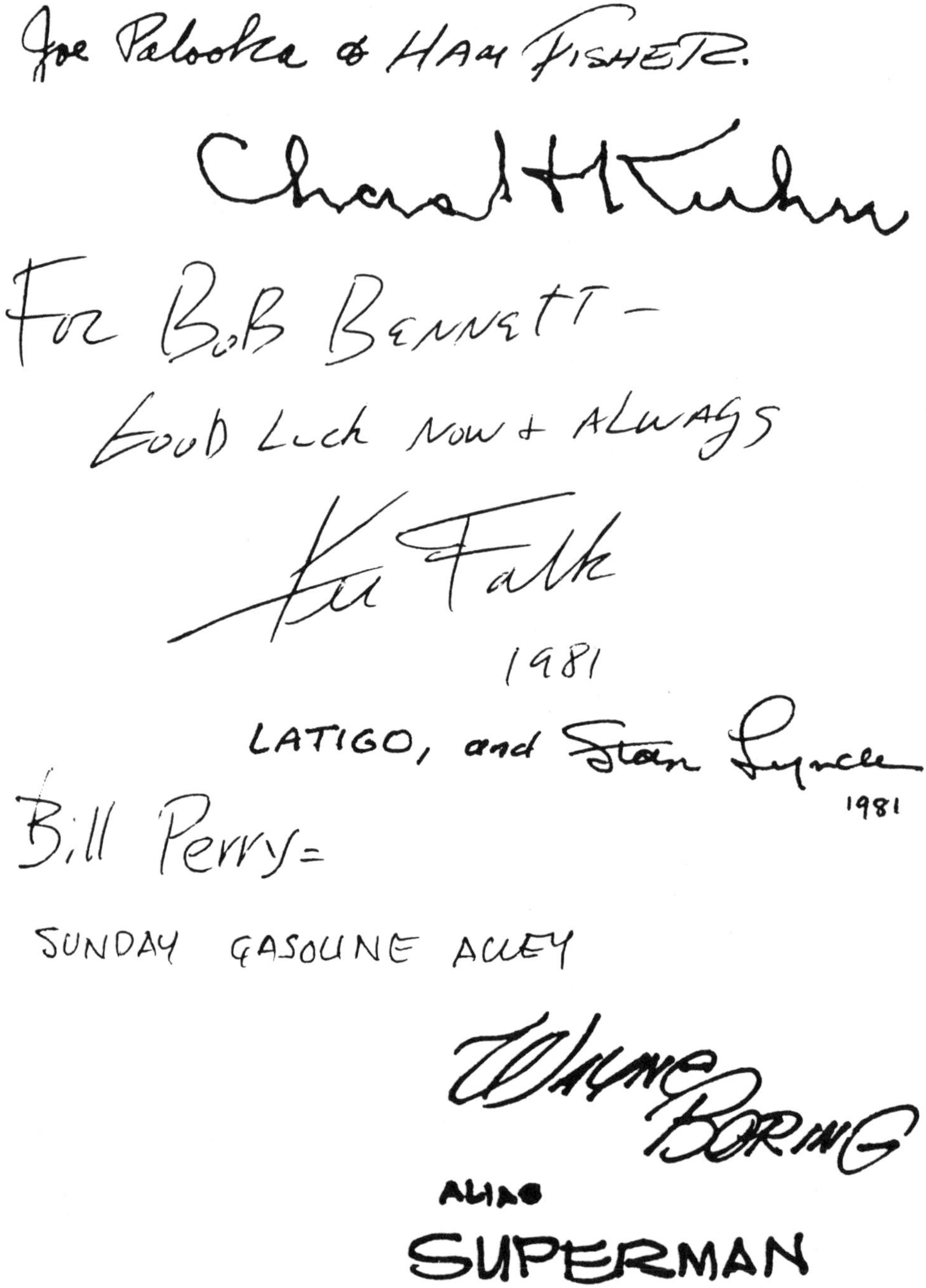

Joe Palooka & HAM FISHER.

Charles H. Kuhn

For Bob Bennett —
Good Luck Now & Always

Lee Falk

1981

LATIGO, and *Stan Lynde*

1981

Bill Perry=

SUNDAY GASOLINE ALLEY

Wayne Boring

ALIAS
SUPERMAN

Ham Fisher ($25), Charles H. Kuhn, Lee Falk, Stan Lynde, Bill Perry, Wayne Boring.

Cartoon voice specialist Mel Blanc, signed photograph with his characters, **$10.** ©1978
Hanna-Barbera Productions, Inc., ©Warner Brothers, Inc. 1978.

Ron Barrett, original drawing of Politenessman, **$10.**

Gene Hazelton, original drawing of Fred Flintstone, **$15.** ©Hanna-Barbera Productions, Inc.

Chris Van Dusen, self-portrait, **$5.**

Bob Clampett, signature with a small sketch, symbolizing his characters Beany and Cecil, **$20.**

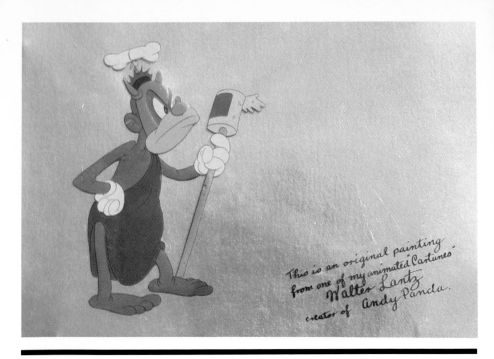

This is an original painting from one of my animated Cartunes. *Walter Lantz* creator of *Andy Panda*.

Animation drawing from an early Walter Lantz cartoon signed by Lantz, **$125.** ©1986 Walter Lantz Productions, Inc.

Animation cel of Spike, **$125.** ©Metro-Goldwyn-Mayer, Inc.

Walter Lantz, original drawing of Woody Woodpecker, **$20.** ©1986 Walter Lantz Productions, Inc.

Animation cel of a dog from an early Warner Brothers Merrie Melodie cartoon, **$100.** ©Warner Brothers, Inc.

Hank Ketcham, original watercolor painting of Dennis the Menace, **$75.** ©Hank Ketcham 1985.

Bud Sagendorf, printed drawing of Popeye the Sailor, hand-colored and signed, **$20.**
Reprinted with special permission of King Features Syndicate, Inc.

Dr. Seuss, original drawing of The Cat in the Hat, **$75.** ©1986 Theodor Seuss Geisel.

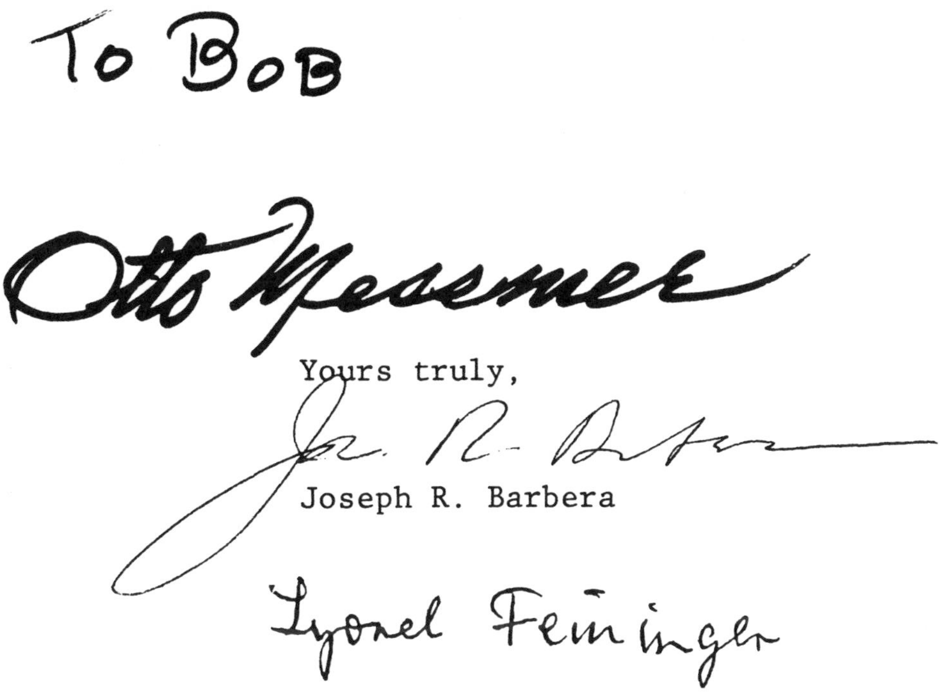
To Bob
Otto Messmer
Yours truly,
Joseph R. Barbera
Lyonel Feininger

Otto Messmer, Joseph R. Barbera, Lyonel Feininger (**$40**).

By advertising your material for sale in the same publications that you shop in, you should have no trouble selling unwanted items as long as your prices are realistic. Remember that other sellers are advertising in the same publications, so you will face stiff competition. Keep in mind that truly important, rare, and valuable items should be sold at auction in order to realize the best price. To sell at auction, contact one of the auction houses listed in the Appendix of this book and send a good description or photocopy of your item. If the auction firm accepts your material, they will notify you of their terms and commission rates. Both very distinguished auction houses, and some which handle less expensive material, are listed in the Appendix. You should choose a firm based on the quality of material you wish to sell as well as on the amount you may actually net. As the hobby grows in popularity, selling material that you no longer desire will become easier. But be careful. As with buying autographs, the economy and the state of the hobby will provide you with information concerning the right time to part with your collection.

Bill Holman, sketch of Smokey Stover, $50.

Chuck Thorndike, $5.

Besides buying cartoon art, you can also obtain many interesting items on your own, often inexpensively. By collecting through the mail—writing to cartoonists and asking for artwork—it is possible to greatly improve your collection and obtain hundreds of unique items. The extremely rare and valuable pieces of cartoon art are seldom found in this manner, but if you have a limited amount of money to spend on your collection, the mail probably is your best resource. If you are on a limited budget, chances are that you will not be able to purchase the most expensive items anyway.

Collecting through the mail can also provide you with many new opportunities. It can introduce you to some of the great cartoonists and animators and, as a result, help you learn more about the talents and skills cartooning demands. A few collectors have even become friends with famous cartoonists, and a number of collectors who have concentrated their collections on material available through the mail have found the hobby more enjoyable and rewarding than mere buying and selling, or even attending an auction.

Mail to almost all authors can be addressed in care of their publishers. If a cartoonist has compiled a book of his cartoons as, for example, Jim Davis has done with *Garfield,* the cartoonist can be written in care of the publisher's address. Also, an illustrator of a book can usually be reached via his or her publisher. Just make sure that the illustrator is still living, the book is not old and out-dated, the publisher exists, and will forward mail to the person you are writing to.

Woody Allen, by Stu Hawple, **$5.**

Comic strip artists can be written to in care of the syndicators who distribute their cartoons, or who distributed the cartoons before the artist's retirement. The name of the syndicator nearly always is provided within the strip itself, as published in your local newspaper. Addresses of all syndicators are found in *Editor And Publisher* magazine, and a list of major syndicator addresses can be found in the Appendix of this book. In the past, the syndicators have been extremely conscientious about forwarding mail to the cartoonists, but this may change in the future if certain cartoonists are besieged with requests for autographs or signed sketches. Already, a few syndicators have refused to forward mail to some of the very popular cartoonists, usually those who have books on the bestseller list. Presently, however, the best way to write to a comic strip artist, short of their business or home address, is in care of their syndicator.

Writing to animators is a little more difficult than to comic strip artists since there is seldom any office or agency that will forward mail to them. Addressing the movie studio is rarely successful as it is almost never forwarded. One good way to reach an animator is to write to their production company. Many of the more renowned animators of the forties and fifties have started these companies to produce commercials and other animated films since the movie cartoon lost its importance after the 1950s. Other animators, such as Ralph Bakshi and Friz Freleng, started production companies to make feature-length or television cartoons. The addresses for these companies can be found in film directories and annuals that are available in larger libraries. In addition,

many production companies are listed in the Yellow pages of the Los Angeles area phone book, also available in your library. Most production companies include the name of the famous animator in their title, such as "Ralph Bakshi Productions." If you cannot find a production company for a particular animator, you will probably have to locate their home address. Surprisingly, a few of these can also be found in the phone book. Another possible source is the *Who's Who* directory.

You may write to magazine and newspaper cartoonists in care of the publications in which their work appears. *The New Yorker, Playboy,* or *Mad,* are usually very good about forwarding your letters. The same is true for editorial and political cartoonists. However, when writing to these cartoonists, make sure that your letter is addressed to the newspaper that distributes their work, and not necessarily the newspaper in which the cartoon appears. You may find a cartoon by political cartoonist Patrick Oliphant in *The New York Times.* However, in order to get your letter to Oliphant, it must be sent to *The Washington Post* where he works. This information is usually provided in fine print within the cartoon.

Home addresses for famous cartoonists are also available, and sources for these addresses are listed in chapter 6. In addition to providing cartoonist's addresses, these sources also feature addresses of personalities in many other fields that can be of use in obtaining celebrity self-portraits by mail. Usually, only major cartoonists can be located through home address listings, so this can pose a problem for you if you are intent on collecting material from many of the lesser known comic strip or animation artists.

Comic book artist Milt Neil, sketch of Howdy Doody, **$20.**

Once you have located the addresses, you must decide what to request of a cartoonist in your letter. Many cartoonists also are collectors of original cartoon art themselves, and they may be reluctant to part with some of their original strips or animation drawings. It will take a very well-written and polite letter to the cartoonist to acquire this kind of material. A few cartoonists will sell their material, but it is best to hold back on this request until you have exhausted all other possibilities for receiving a free drawing. Most cartoonists are very receptive to honest collectors in search of originals. If they feel you are trying to gain material only for purposes of re-sale, they will ignore your request.

If it is not possible to send original strips or actual animation drawings, many cartoonists will send you a signed sketch of their character if you write them a polite and courteous letter, and enclose a self-addressed, stamped envelope. It is also advisable to send the cartoonist a 3″ by 5″ card or an 8½″ by 11″ sheet of drawing paper, along with an appropriately sized return envelope, to assist the cartoonist in complying with your request. It is not a good idea to ask the cartoonist for several drawings: keep your request to one or two small sketches, or one large sketch. Otherwise, you are likely to receive nothing at all. Although a few cartoonists will only send you their signature, most are receptive to making a sketch—at least under the right set of circumstances— i.e., a polite and respectful request letter.

You might also consider asking the cartoonist an interesting question regarding his or her work if you are interested in the history of comic strips or animation. A nice letter from a cartoonist in response to your question would be a fine addition to your collection, and may even be framed and matted with an original sketch or animation drawing. Again, when asking a question of a cartoonist, as in requesting an original sketch, make sure that your letter is courteous and that you have enclosed a self-addressed, stamped envelope.

There are just a few other things to remember when composing your letter. Type it, if at all possible; keep it short and sincere; and, if you have any doubts about return postage, call the Post Office. They will be most happy to advise you in the matter. Even though a cartoonist may owe a measure of gratitude to those who read his strip, this debt does not include original artwork. When writing to a cartoonist living in a foreign country, send International Reply Coupons (available at the Post Office) instead of stamps, so that the cartoonist will have an easier time responding to your letter. The Post Office will tell you how many coupons you will need for your return envelope.

Some cartoonists simply will not respond to a request for original artwork through the mail no matter how wonderful your letter is. A much larger group of cartoonists will respond to the polite request, but some of these artists are very selective about sending their original artwork to collectors. They seem to fear that collectors are asking for drawings only to turn around and sell the drawings to others. To allay these fears, and to obtain originals from some of the more unwilling cartoonists, try to impress upon the cartoonist that you are a serious collector of cartoon art, working to build an important and significant collection. You might consider listing a few of the important items already in your collection in your letter. A cartoonist is much more likely to send original art to a collector who is building and preserving a collection of museum-like quality.

Rowland B. Wilson, $10.

There are few problems associated with obtaining cartoon art through the mail, but one that you may encounter concerns the authenticity of the material you receive. The most usual type of unauthentic artwork sent to collectors is the pre-printed cartoon. Many cartoonists and animators who lack the time to make original drawings for collectors will often send printed copies of their drawings that they will sometimes authentically sign. Printer's ink is dull and lacks color and weight variations so it is not difficult to determine whether a cartoon drawing is pre-printed. Real ink, in contrast, is shiny, shaded, and contains color and weight variations. These unauthentic drawings seldom fool collectors and really pose no significant problem.

The major problem involving unau-thentic cartoon art is whether the drawing was actually made by the cartoonist, or was instead drawn by an assistant. A large number of the well-established cartoonists have assistants who help to produce their strips, sometimes even drawing the strip themselves. Hank Ketcham, the creator of "Dennis the Menace," handles the artwork for the daily Dennis cartoons while his two assistants draw Dennis for the Sunday edition of your paper. Similar circumstances exist for animators. In the making of an animated cartoon, hundreds, or even thousands, of artists take part, and all are skilled in drawing the major character of the cartoon. If you write to an animator who has his own production company, there is no guarantee that any drawing you receive will have been made by that particular animator. And if you ask an animator for a cel from a finished cartoon, it is most unlikely that the cel will be one drawn by the animator. Walt Disney, as well as most animators of classic Hollywood cartoons, never animated a single cel used in the production of any cartoon.

Although cartoon art produced by an assistant does have value, it carries much less value than artwork by a famous animator or cartoonist. And when you write to a recognized cartoonist expecting one of his or her original sketches, and receive one drawn by an assistant, there is good reason to be disappointed. Unfortunately, unless the cartoonist has a very distinctive touch, it is nearly impossible to discern his or her drawings from those of an assistant. A cartoonist's signature on the artwork may provide an indication of whether or not the work is his, although this alone does not mean that he or she drew it. Signature comparison, however, is probably the best thing you can work with. Compare the signature on your drawing to the artist's signature on a newspaper strip. If it matches well, it usually means that the cartoonist took the time to make the drawing as well, especially if the drawing is a quick sketch, rather than something elaborate.

There is seldom a sure way to tell whether a piece of cartoon artwork was actually drawn by the cartoonist or an assistant and the answer usually depends upon the material in question. Animation cels are almost always staff work. The exceptions to this rule are cartoonists who started out as assistants, such as Chuck Jones, or Hank Ketcham. Even if a cel is signed by a famous animator, it is still unlikely that the animator drew it.

Recently a few signed cels and watercolors of Disney characters, bearing Disney's authentic signature, appeared on the market. Although these were sold for very high prices, the drawings were not made by Disney and they were not represented as the work of Disney by the sellers. Original cartoon strips are usually the work of the person who signed the strip with some exceptions. If the strip is very popular and time-consuming, or the signer of the strip is older and near retirement, the chance of it being drawn by an assistant is much greater. If the strip is produced by a studio, such as Disney's newspaper strips, it probably is the work of an assistant or a group of them. Original sketches are almost always the work of the cartoonist they were solicited from.

In many ways the value of artwork produced by assistants and famous cartoonists is determined by people's expectations about the item. People do not expect a cel to have been drawn by anyone famous, so the fact that an assistant drew it doesn't affect price. A cel has value because it may have great beauty, or because it played an important role in the animation process. People do, however, expect original sketches to be the actual work of the cartoonist whose name appears on the drawing. If one was drawn by an assistant instead, it has much less value.

Collecting cartoon art is a fun chore, and the difficulties peculiar to the hobby should not prove too challenging. Be a careful and skeptical buyer and take the time to acquaint yourself with prices. And if you wish to build your collection by writing to cartoonists for original artwork, you should be able to assemble a very valuable collection at a minimum of expense.

2 Animation Art

Of all the various specialties in collecting cartoon art, animation art is among the most interesting and unique. Aside from the lasting contribution that animation has made to the cinema and popular culture, it has fathered collectible works of far greater diversity than any other area of cartooning. Furthermore, the materials used in the production of animated films, from storyboards to watercolor background paintings, are not only works of art but also highly sought after movie memorabilia. Animation art is very difficult to collect, but carefully selected items in this category make wonderful display items and offer exciting investment opportunities for the knowledgeable collector.

If you are interested in collecting animation art, it is a good idea to acquaint yourself with the history of animation as well as the type of art available from different time periods in animation's history.

Most film historians trace the beginning of animated cartoons back to 1909 when comic strip artist Winsor McCay first presented his animated film, *Gertie the Dinosaur*. Yet, animation existed in similar forms before that time, specifically in the work of the Frenchman, Emile Cohl, and the American, J. Stuart Blackton. The inspiration for these films can be traced to a variety of sources. A most

Winsor McCay, creator of the first animated cartoon, **\$250.**

important influence was the comic strip, which was steadily gaining in popularity. For years, flip-books, and devices such as the zoetrope, were marketed in an attempt to make the comics move, and the medium of film fulfilled this goal. Innovative filmmaking, such as the work of George Melies in France, was also instrumental in producing the first animated cartoons.

Early animated films were largely the work of comic strip artists who entered the medium of film. Winsor McCay, who drew the brilliant strip, "Little Nemo," was a very well-established comic strip artist before he plunged into animation. Well-known cartoonists of the period, such as George McManus, Milt Gross, and Rube Goldberg, also became involved in making films in animation's early period.

In the early animated cartoons, the animator performed the extremely painstaking task of making every drawing that went into the production of a cartoon, including all of the backgrounds that were drawn with each frame of film. When Winsor McCay made an animated film of Little Nemo, he animated four thousand drawings, and hand-colored the 35mm frames so that his film would have a color tint. Since making animated films in this manner proved very costly and time consuming, several animators searched for an alternative method. The first step in simplifying the animation process was achieved by John Randolph Bray in 1914. Bray printed copies of backgrounds on translucent paper and placed these over blank sheets of paper, so that only the part of the scene requiring movement would need to be drawn each time.

Bray later improved this technique by adding gray tones to animated drawings where before only black and white line drawings were used.

The most important innovation in animation technique, however, was the work of another early animator, Earl Hurd. Hurd was the inventor of the celluloid process (later shortened to "cel"—a name given to an animation drawing on celluloid). This process involved inking characters on transparent sheets placed on top of stationary background drawings. Over the years Hurd's methods were refined, usually by some of the giants of animation such as Walt Disney and Max Fleischer, but the process is still used today in substantially the same form.

The animated cartoon became very popular during the 1920s, largely due to the success of the character, Felix the Cat, and the films of the Fleischer brothers. Felix the Cat was one of the first important animated characters to begin his career in films rather than in the comics, although he later appeared in comic form. Most of the earlier animated cartoons featured comic strip characters such as George Herriman's Krazy Kat and Bud Fisher's Mutt and Jeff.

Although Felix the Cat is often associated with newspaper cartoonist Pat Sullivan, Sullivan took only a small part in the creation of the character. Felix was created at Sullivan's animation studio in Fort Lee, New Jersey, by Otto Messmer. Messmer produced the entire series of Felix cartoons almost single-handedly, and later even drew most of the strips for the newspaper. The Felix films were among the first cartoons to gather a great deal of critical acclaim, and they were even compared to the work of famed silent comedians, such as Chaplin and Keaton. Even today, the Felix films are highly regarded. *New York Times* film critic, Vincent Canby, upon viewing a revival program of Felix cartoons, wrote that in these films, "The freedom of the form looks almost avant-garde." Although the Felix character was revived by another studio in the 1930s, and for television cartoons in the 1960s, the original films remain far superior.

Probably the most successful and innovative animators of the 1920s were Max and Dave Fleischer. The Fleischers were responsible for creating Betty Boop and Koko the Clown, both popular 1920's characters, and also for their revolutionary filmmaking techniques. The early Fleischer films, featuring a mixture of live action and animation, were masterful in their cinematic approach. The animation itself was made much more realistic than ever before through a device known as the "rotoscope." This device projected films of live actors, frame-by-frame, onto a drawing board, where life-like images of characters were drawn. The Fleischers also pioneered a 3-D process, which added a feeling of depth to an animated film. Both this process, and the rotoscope, were later used successfully by Walt Disney in producing his feature-length classics.

As Walt Disney and other animators gained prominence, however, the Fleischers were gradually reduced to being followers, instead of leaders, in producing animated films. Although they continued making cartoons into the 1940s, including the feature-length *Gulliver's Travels*, (1939), and series featuring the comic characters Popeye and Superman, the 1920s was probably their most productive period.

Felix the Cat by creator Otto Messmer, **$85.** Reprinted with special permission of King Features Syndicate, Inc.

Koko the Clown by Max Fleischer, **$175.**

Sketches of the "spies" from the 1939 Max Fleischer feature cartoon *Gulliver's Travels,* by animator Bill Sturm, **$20.**

The Fleischer versions of Popeye and Olive Oyl, by animator Bill Sturm, **$25.** Reprinted with special permission by King Features Syndicate, Inc.

Animation cel from *Gulliver's Travels,* signed by Dave Fleischer, **$125.**

Animation materials from the Fleischer cartoons are fairly scarce, although a few cels and preliminary sketches of characters are sometimes available, at prices not less than $100. Max and Dave Fleischer both died in the 1970s, but quite a few animators who worked with them are still alive. These include *National Lampoon* cartoonist Leslie Cabarga, as well as Shamus Culhane and Seymour Kneitel, who also worked for several other animation studios through the 1940s and 1950s.

The most famous and brilliant animator ever, Walt Disney, began filming cartoons in the 1920s. Disney was actually more of a great businessman than a great cartoonist since, unlike the animators that came before him, he realized that animated films could reach heights never before imagined, and would someday be regarded as serious films. Disney was responsible for many of the innovations in animated films, including sound and a high-quality technicolor process. But more importantly, Disney revolutionized

Walt Disney and his wife. Photograph signed by Mrs. Disney, **$10.**

extremely valuable. The Disney studio has carefully guarded most of the original material, but cels, drawings, and paintings of Disney characters are not too difficult to locate, although expensive. A cel used in a Disney feature was sold for as much as $18,000, although it is possible to obtain Disney material at much lower prices. An average cel featuring Donald Duck, for instance, sells for under $200. And an extremely important Disney item, a set of pencil drawings used in the production of *Snow White*, recently sold for just over $2,000 at an auction of animation art.

Original drawings of characters, made by Disney himself, are very hard to locate. Disney could draw, however, and he started his career as a proficient commercial artist. His handwritten letters from this period, frequently filled with sketches, appear on the market quite regularly. Yet, when Disney first established his animation studio, he employed more talented artists to do the actual drawing and devoted his energies to perfecting the animation process and merchandising his characters. Several legends abound regarding the creation of famous Disney characters, such as one about a mouse that Disney supposedly spotted during a train trip, giving him the inspiration for Mickey Mouse. In reality, Mickey was created by Disney animator Ub Iwerks in 1928, who also almost single-handedly drew the first Mickey Mouse cartoon, *Plane Crazy*. Although Disney may have made sketches of Mickey Mouse, or other characters, during his lifetime, he rarely sketched anything for collectors and seldom even took the time to send his authentic autograph. Disney's studio artists, including Hank Porter and

animation. In the silent era, animators were preoccupied with gags, slapstick, and with "making the comics move." Disney's earlier work was similar to these efforts, but he later went far beyond his original successes by using the medium to make brilliant feature-length masterpieces, such as *Snow White and the Seven Dwarfs* (1937) and the classic *Fantasia* (1940). Disney's short subjects, featuring his famous characters Mickey Mouse, Donald Duck, Goofy, and others, also showed a high degree of artistic skill, as Disney was committed to excellence in his every endeavor. If it were not for Disney, animation might never have received the critical respect and universal admiration that it has.

Due to the unmatched success and the brilliant achievements of the Disney studio, Disney animation art is in very great demand, and has become

Secretarial and authentic signatures of Walt Disney:

Secretarial signature, probably by Floyd Gottfredson.

Secretarial signature by Bob Moore.

Secretarial signature, probably by Hank Porter.

Secretarial signature by a Disney studio artist.

SINCERELY,
WALT DISNEY

Floyd Gottfredson, took turns answering Disney's fan mail, and they also signed and drew Disney newspaper strips. Sketches and paintings of Disney characters, bearing authentic Disney signatures, have appeared on the market at substantial prices (usually starting at $1,000), but there has been no attempt to credit the art to Disney.

In addition to animated cels, storyboards, model sheets, and preliminary drawings of Disney characters, original sketches of characters made by Disney animators are readily available and are not difficult to obtain, even by mail. These include Hank Ketcham (creator of "Dennis the Menace"); Ward Kimball (a Disney animator and one of his "nine old men"); distinguished magazine cartoonist Eldon Dedini; and Carl Barks, who drew Donald Duck for the comic strips. Barks' work, in particular, has sold for very high prices as he was a masterful artist. A painting by Barks of Uncle Scrooge recently sold for $35,000 at an auction, and there have been reports that similar works by Barks have sold for much more. An excellent book reprinting hundreds of Disney animation materials is Frank Thomas' and Ollie Johnston's _Disney Animation: The Illusion of Life_ (1984). Both Thomas and Johnston were key Disney animators during the prime of the Disney studio.

When Disney animation reached its peak in the 1930s and 1940s, many other animation studios stepped up their efforts, and a classic and fruitful period in Hollywood animation was launched. Most of the major film studios featured animation departments, as animated cartoons were shown along with feature films in the theatres. Of all the cartoon studios of the 1930s and 1940s, however, three towered above the rest: Warner Brothers, MGM, and Walter Lantz.

Disney animator Ward Kimball, **$20.**

Many of the finest and funniest cartoons produced in the forties and fifties originated in the Warner Brothers animation unit. For sheer humor, no studio approached Warners, not even Disney's. And Warner's most famous character, Bugs Bunny, surpassed Mickey Mouse and other Disney characters in popularity.

Warner Brothers began making cartoons in the early 1930s, and two of the earliest Warner animators were Rudy Ising and Hugh Harman, refugees from the Disney studio. It wasn't until the mid-1930s, however, that the studio began to experiment with new ideas and characters and to grow in popularity. Warners assembled a group of young and inventive animation directors, including Bob Clampett, Tex Avery, Chuck Jones and Friz Freleng, and gave them free rein over the production process, albeit with limited budgets.

Virtually nothing was sacred to these Warner directors and almost every single one of their cartoons proved to be a comic gem. Those who worked at Warners in the thirties and forties pursued their goal of outcompeting Disney with almost single-minded devotion. Although they did not exactly accomplish this goal, they made many extraordinary films with fresh and different characters. Bugs Bunny, in particular, proved to be not only a very popular character, but a constant source of wisecracking humor as well. Unfortunately, much of the humor in the early Warner cartoons featured a good deal of racial stereotyping—an attitude prevalent in both cartoons and feature films of that era.

Animation materials from Warner Brothers can be found without difficulty and are not enormously expensive. Prices for the average cel featuring Bugs Bunny, Daffy Duck, or

BEST TO BOB
FROM
Friz Freleng

Sketches of the Pink Panther and Bugs Bunny by animator Friz Freleng, **$15.** Pink Panther ©DePatie-Freleng, Inc., Bugs Bunny ©Warner Brothers, Inc.

Porky Pig start at around $100 depending upon the age and the importance of the drawing. Much of the material used in the making of the Warner cartoons was saved by the late Bob Clampett, but quite a bit was also lost or destroyed. One tremendous source of reprinted Warner material, is *Tex Avery* (1986), a magnificent book by Frenchman Patrick Brion. Avery himself, like Jones and Freleng, never bothered to collect or save many originals, and gave away dozens of drawings to children who waited at his house and pestered him for them.

Tex Avery was perhaps the greatest comic genius associated with animated cartoons, and his original artwork is in great demand and very valuable. Avery played an important part in developing the personality of Bugs Bunny, and other Warner characters, but moved over to MGM in the early forties. MGM is known primarily today for William Hanna and Joseph Barbera's Tom and Jerry characters, but Avery's films outshone virtually all of MGM's efforts with the possible exception of the Tom and Jerry classics. While working for MGM, Avery proved that he was not only a great animator and gagman, but also a superior filmmaker who challenged the conventions of the cartoon. For example, one of his cartoons featured a character who lost a leg at the beginning of the cartoon, and spent the rest of the film searching for it. Another presented characters involved in a chase scene who decided to stop chasing each other and sit down to discuss alternative endings for the film. His cartoons were replète with verbal and visual puns, and as films they were similar to the work of filmmakers such as Eisenstein, Hitchcock, or Bunuel, in their use of various cinematic devices.

Bugs Bunny by Chuck Jones, **$25.** ©Warner Brothers, Inc.

Animator's pencil sketches of Bugs Bunny
and Daffy Duck by animator Friz Freleng.
$15 each. ©Warner Brothers, Inc.

Avery's films, however, totally lacked
any sort of pretentiousness. It is no
wonder that today Avery is revered in
Europe, and that his cartoons are often
shown in programs featuring European and American experimental or
artistic films.

Most of the other MGM films were
very different from Avery's, but were
of very high quality. The MGM Tom
and Jerry cartoons were high budget
films, and sometimes featured beautiful oil paintings, rather than the usual
watercolor backgrounds. These and
other MGM animation materials claim
fairly high prices if and when they can
be located.

Another fine animator who began
working in the silent era was Walter
Lantz. Lantz originally made films
similar to those of Max Fleischer, but,
as his studio grew, he developed his
own style, and characters such as
Woody Woodpecker and Andy Panda
were eventually created. Lantz's
characters, like Disney's, were essen-
tially studio products, but Lantz is a
fine artist who is also very generous in
sending original sketches to collectors.
Animation materials from his studio
are not very hard to find and prices are
fairly reasonable.

Warner Brothers animator Bob Clampett, signed photograph, **$20.**

Walter Lantz surrounded by his many cartoon creations, **$15.** ©1986 Walter Lantz Productions, Inc.

Besides the studios and animators we have mentioned, several other filmmakers released cartoons during Hollywood's golden age of animation in the thirties and forties. These included Paul Terry's Terrytoons, featuring Mighty Mouse and Heckle and Jeckle, and the UPA studios who produced Mr. Magoo and Gerald McBoing Boing cartoons. UPA was responsible for many stylistic changes in the cartoon, especially in backgrounds and in design. Original material from both of these studios, and virtually any other of the period, are also worth purchasing.

After the 1950s, the animated movie cartoon declined in popularity. One of the major reasons for this decline was that the movie studios stopped releasing cartoons along with feature films, and, as a result, budgets for animated short subjects became nonexistent. Yet, the cartoon survived via the medium of television. Television cartoons, due to limited budgets, never matched the quality of their movie counterparts, but many have provided a certain amount of humor and other enjoyable moments. Animation material of television cartoons is also much easier to find than similar material from movie cartoons, and it is much less expensive as well. The average cel from a television cartoon is normally priced at around $25. Original sketches of characters are very plentiful as well, since many of the animators working on television cartoons are still living.

Hanna-Barbera Studios have produced the most successful television cartoons. They created Tom and Jerry at MGM and started producing their own cartoons in the late 1950s. The major reason for their success was that they were able to work with limited

Woody Woodpecker by Walter Lantz, **$20.** © 1986 Walter Lantz Productions, Inc.

British animator John Halas, who directed the 1954 film, *Animal Farm,* based on George Orwell's novel, original sketch, **$15.**

Mr. Magoo by creator Stephen Bosustow, $25.

budgets. Movement in these cartoons was kept to a bare minimum, and much of the animation was provided by computer and photocopying techniques. Nevertheless, the studio did produce some enjoyable series and characters, including Huckleberry Hound, The Jetsons, and The Flintstones. The latter series was based both on the popular television show, "The Honeymooners," and on a Tex Avery cartoon from the 1950s, "The First Bad Man," in which western conventions were transferred to prehistoric times. "The Flintstones" began as a top-rated, prime time series, and originally offered some social commentary as well as humor.

Besides the work of Hanna and Barbera, there were a few other well-produced television cartoon series. Perhaps the finest of these was Jay Ward's "Rocky and Bullwinkle Show," that debuted in the late 1950s. This series offered a sometimes bizarre collection of puns, which often appealed more to adults than to children. Friz Freleng's "The Pink Panther," which

began as a lead-in to the Blake Edwards films, also became a popular series with some appeal to adults.

If you are seriously collecting animation materials and would like the television cartoon represented in your collection, it is best to collect material from the most recognizable and popular series and avoid material from most of today's Saturday morning fare. Remember, material with lasting appeal and some historical significance makes the best investment.

Our survey of animation and animated cartoons has dealt primarily with the work of major Hollywood studios where most material currently on the market originated. It must be mentioned, however, that Hollywood is not the only source of animated film. All through Hollywood's golden era of animation, and continuing today, foreign studios produced hundreds of shorts and feature films, some similar to the Hollywood product, and others wildly different, fresh, and experimental. We have also overlooked recent Hollywood feature length cartoons,

Norman Maurer, animator of The Three Stooges cartoons, $15.

such as the work of Ralph Bakshi (animator of the films "Fritz the Cat" and "American Pop"). Animation materials from the great majority of these films are well worth collecting, and can add an unusual dimension to your collection. This material is difficult to find since many animators and studios are located in Europe. Addresses are hard to come by, and not many local sellers handle these items.

There is a wide variety of animation materials on the market, and a thorough knowledge of exactly what is available and its role in producing a cartoon is essential. Also, investors will want to understand the relative values of the various animation materials.

The use of the cel in making cartoons developed over a period of time. When purchasing animation material dated prior to 1925, remember that, more often than not, drawings were inked on paper rather than on transparent sheets. In addition, earlier animation drawings included everything that would appear in a frame of film—such as backgrounds or additional, stationary characters. These early animation drawings are very valuable for their age and scarcity. Early drawings were more elaborate than cel drawings, since on a cel, only one charac-

ter (or sometimes only parts of a character, as in the Hanna-Barbera cartoons) usually appears. In earlier days, the animators usually made all of the drawings that went into the production of a cartoon. Winsor McCay produced the artwork for his Little Nemo cartoon, and Ub Iwerks single-handedly animated the first Mickey Mouse cartoon, *Plane Crazy*. Drawings made by famous animators are almost always worth more than those made by assistants, unless, of course, the drawing itself is in greater demand.

The development of the cel paved the way for the mass production of animated cartoons, but other technological changes and a greater demand for cartoon films further improved production techniques. In the 1930s, animation studios began employing hundreds of assistants to animate characters on cels, and the directors and animators of cartoons from that time onward seldom performed this work themselves. The thirties also introduced the color cartoon, when Walter Lantz animated a technicolor sequence for the 1930 Bing Crosby musical, *King of Jazz*. Several studios continued making black and white films for several years until 1940 when most of them responded to the color demand.

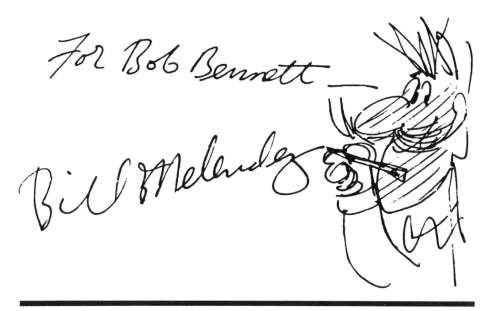

Bill Melendez, animator of the "Peanuts" television specials, self-portrait, $10.

Although the most famous animators seldom animated characters on cels after the silent period, they continued to play an active role in the production of their cartoons. The job of an animator involves working with scriptwriters to produce a storyboard, and working with animation assistants to insure that characters are drawn uniformly and to precise specifications. The processes involved in making a cartoon yield different types of artwork, and this artwork, although offered for sale at infrequent intervals, is available if you take the time to look for it.

A storyboard sketch is usually made by an animator or director in consultation with a scriptwriter. When grouped together, these sketches serve to guide the filmmaking crew by featuring key scenes in the cartoon, revealing plot developments, providing instruction, and indicating backgrounds. Storyboard sketches are usually rough, drawn with pencil or charcoals, and they range in size from about 3″ by 5″ to about 11″ by 17″. Depending on size and elaboration, a storyboard sketch can bring a high price, although this also depends on the importance of the film and scarcity.

A model sheet is usually more desirable than a storyboard sketch. Model sheets contain several sketches of characters, usually in pencil, and also include directions regarding relative proportions. These drawings provide working instructions to animation assistants, who must duplicate the work of the animator. In order to provide this assistance, a model sheet pictures a character in several different poses, and includes an entire range of possible facial expressions. Model sheets show considerably more depth than quick sketches or average cels and are seen as more desirable by collectors. Also, a model sheet has value because it serves an important role in making an animated film.

Ralph Bakshi, animator of Robert Crumb's "Fritz the Cat," self-portrait, $20.

Model sheets and storyboard sketches are not the only drawings made by animators rather than assistants in the production of a cartoon. The animator must make other sketches and drawings, both to experiment with certain characters and poses, and to establish the extremes of a character's movement.

Even before beginning production of a storyboard, an animator may want to experiment with the designs of certain characters. Many famous cartoon characters, notably Woody Woodpecker and Bugs Bunny, have undergone major changes in design and development, and an animator may decide to alter the appearance of a character for a particular project. In originally designing a character, of course, a great deal of experimentation is also necessary. In making Walt Disney's *Pinnochio*, animators scrapped several different designs for the main character before they were satisfied with his appearance. Most of the time, however, preliminary or experimental drawings are used only for slight alterations in a character's appearance, or for designing other elements of a cartoon, such as costumes or scenery.

Once a character is designed, and a storyboard has been completed, the job of the animator continues. Thousands of drawings are used to make an animated film, and most of these drawings are made by animation assistants. Yet, the animator of a film must make the key drawings, those that establish extremes of movement, in order to simplify the task of his assistants. Once these essential drawings have been made, it then becomes the task of the assistants to produce the rest of the drawings necessary to complete a film.

Preliminary sketches by animators are usually difficult to find and are far less plentiful than animation drawings. Both are usually pencil drawings, but are easily distinguished from storyboard sketches since they lack background scenery.

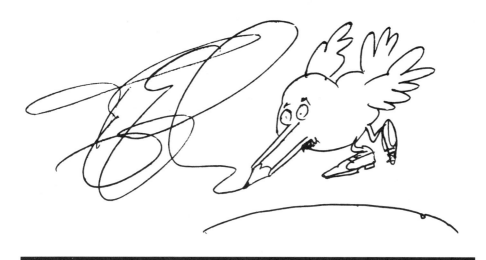

Terry Gilliam, animator of the "Monty Python" cartoons, and creator of the movie *Brazil*, original drawing, **$25.**

Animation backgrounds are wonderful additions to a collection of animation art. Since they are usually high-quality paintings, they make unusual display items. Probably the most innovative backgrounds are those used in the making of experimental cartoons, or those designed by the UPA animation studios in the 1950s. UPA revolutionized cartoon design, especially backgrounds, and examples of their work could provide excellent investment opportunities if you are able to locate it.

Most animation backgrounds are watercolors, but some have been produced in oils such as the MGM backgrounds for the Tom and Jerry cartoons. They are strikingly beautiful, fairly scarce, and very expensive. Very few animation backgrounds are available for less than $75.

For a further study of animation materials we suggest *Tex Avery* (1986) by Patrick Brion, and *Disney Animation: The Illusion of Life* (1984) by Frank Thomas and Ollie Johnston.

Original sketches and paintings, made by animators for collectors, are not part of the animation process, but are nonetheless valuable and worthy of collecting. Quick sketches made by animators are most common. Many were obtained in person on album pages, but the great majority on the market were obtained by mail. There are several good reasons to collect original sketches—they are inexpensive, plentiful, and easy to obtain. Furthermore, they are generally made by famous individuals, which increases their value. Although they lack the beauty of animated cels, they nevertheless make fine display items. Prices for average sketches by living animators range from $10 to $25, while prices for sketches by deceased animators can range all the way from $15 to $100.

You may write to animators and request a signed sketch (as described in chapter 1), or you can buy signed sketches from an autograph dealer. Dealers who sell animated cels and

67

other animation materials, however, rarely handle original sketches. Chapter 6 deals more with the autograph hobby, and will show you how to contact autograph dealers who specialize in cartoon art.

Original paintings of characters are not common, but occasionally a few will be offered for sale. Fairly elaborate paintings made by famous animators are oftentimes more valuable than any other animation material because a painting takes much longer to complete and has greater detail than a cel. A painting of Mickey Mouse, or another Disney character, by a Disney animator is usually worth upwards of $1,000, and paintings by Carl Barks are worth much more.

Whether you wish to collect original paintings, sketches, or animation materials, you will find that collecting animation art can be very complex at times, but it offers a wide selection of material that is fun to display and has interesting investment potential. Concentrate on collecting the finest quality material, with the most artistic and historical significance, and you should be able to build a first-rate collection.

3 Comic Strips and Books

Comic strip and comic book collectibles have been very popular with collectors for a great many years. Old newspaper strips and rare comic books have been especially popular, but comic collectors have also bought and traded toys, dolls, clothing, and almost any other item related to the comics. It is strange, however, that amidst all of the comic collecting frenzy, original art has been almost completely overlooked. Original comic art consistently brings high prices at sales and auctions, but as of now, only a few comic collectors have pursued this avenue seriously.

One possible reason for this lack of interest is that many collectors consider original comic art unobtainable, or available at prices well beyond their budget. It is true that comic art is generally more scarce than animation art. Thousands of drawings go into the production of an animated cartoon, but for every newspaper strip, there is only one original. Nevertheless, many of the fears collectors have about original comic art are groundless. There are hundreds, even thousands, of strips to collect, and one long-running strip has produced hundreds of originals. Rare or significant strips have brought high prices, but the average daily strip may be purchased for as little as $50, and an average Sunday strip can be had for under $100. Original sketches

Rudolph Dirks, original drawing of The Katzenjammer Kids, **$250.** Reprinted with special permission of King Features Syndicate, Inc.

"Moon Mullins," original strip by Ferd and Tom Johnson, **$75**. Reprinted by permission: Tribune Media Services.

of famous characters sell for as little as $5 to $10, or for the cost of postage if you decide to write to the cartoonists themselves and ask for a drawing. The fact that comic art is unique only makes it a much worthier collectible.

Americans have been fascinated by the comics and with comic collectibles since the turn-of-the-century, but the comic form actually originated in Germany rather than in America. Wilhelm Busch, who began his career as an illustrator and caricaturist, is credited with producing the first comic strip in 1865, featuring his characters Max and Moritz. Busch's work met with little success in his homeland, but it sparked the beginning of comic drawings in Europe and in America. Busch himself wearied of producing comic strips and turned to painting instead. His original paintings, which were not displayed until after his death, are currently valued at over ten million dollars!

Probably the greatest example of Busch's influence is the American strip, "The Katzenjammer Kids," originally drawn by Rudolph Dirks. The characters in this strip looked like Max and Moritz, and many of their adventures were similar. "The Katzenjammer Kids" was one of the first American strips to gain tremendous popularity, and it is one of the most important creations in the history of comic strips.

American cartoonists, however, lagged behind European artists for several years, and the comic strip was well-established in many foreign countries before it appeared in America. One of the earliest American comic strips to appear in print was R. F. Outcault's "The Yellow Kid," which debuted in Joseph Pulitzer's *World* in 1896. "The Yellow Kid" was unlike many of the comic strips that followed,

R.F. Outcault, original drawing of Tige, Buster Brown's dog, **$350.**

but it nevertheless was very influential in the history of the comics. Outcault's original drawings of The Yellow Kid are scarce (only eight are known to exist), and one recently sold for over $15,000 at an auction of comic and illustration art. Besides drawing "The Yellow Kid," Outcault also produced the classic "Buster Brown."

With the success of "The Yellow Kid," newspaper publishers scrambled to bring comic strips to more and more readers. William Randolph Hearst saw great promise in the comic medium, and assembled a legendary group of cartoonists for his papers, including James Swinnerton ("Little Jimmy"), Rudolph Dirks, and Outcault, whom he hired away from Pulitzer.

In addition to these cartoonists, many others began successful strips in the early 1900s, and revolutionized the medium in the process. Among these were Frederick Burr Opper, the creator of the wonderfully comic "Happy Hooligan," the distinguished artists

Winsor McCay and Lyonel Feininger, and Captain Bud Fisher, author of the famous strip "Mutt and Jeff." Of all these early artists, however, it was McCay whose work set new standards for the comics. His artistic talents were unequalled, and only Feininger approached his genius. McCay's originals are highly prized by collectors, and "Little Nemo" strips currently sell for around $4,000 each.

McCay's strips, especially "Little Nemo," are unlike any of today's in appearance. Their simple eloquence and graceful design come closer to fine art than to mere cartoons. But despite McCay's efforts, it was George McManus who set the style and standards for other cartoonists. McManus drew several strips before hitting on "Bringing Up Father," which became his greatest success, and his later work included producing animated cartoons with Emile Cohl. His work in animation never approached his mastery of the newspaper cartoon, however, and though his strips have been widely imitated, they feature a charm and wit that can never be duplicated.

In recent years critics have discovered George Herriman. Herriman's famed character "Krazy Kat" began in 1913, and gradually rivaled McManus' "Bringing Up Father" in popularity. At first glance, "Krazy Kat" seems to be a rather simplistic strip, but a closer look reveals highly developed humor, and even literary genius. Many famous writers and other artists have praised the strip for these reasons, including E. B. White, H. L. Mencken, e. e. cummings, and Walt Disney, while author Jack Kerouac maintained that the strip presaged the Beat Generation. An excellent collection of "Krazy Kat" strips,

WINSOR McCAY

Winsor McCay, original drawing of Little Nemo, **$400.**

as well as the most recent appraisal of Herriman's work, can be found in *Krazy Kat: The Comic Art of George Herriman* (1986) by Karen O'Connell, Georgia Riley deHavenon, and Patrick McDonnell.

Like Opper's "Happy Hooligan," "Krazy Kat" also set new standards for comic strip humor that were followed by artists such as Milt Gross and Rube Goldberg. Goldberg was one of the great comic geniuses of the newspaper cartoon, and his strips featuring his famous inventions ("Rube Goldberg contraptions") rank as some of the funniest ever produced. Gross' strips were also filled with wacky humor, and this trend dominated the comics throughout the 1910s and 1920s.

Besides Gross and Goldberg, many other cartoonists helped to establish this period as one of the most creative and productive in the history of the comics. Classic strips, such as Cliff Sterrett's "Polly and Her Pals," Fontaine Fox's "Toonerville Folks," Billy DeBeck's "Barney Google" and Segar's "Thimble Theatre" (featuring the famous character, Popeye), won wide audiences, and reached new highs in humor and artistry. Ferd Johnson, who started working in the comics in 1923 and is now the oldest active comic artist, recalls that these cartoonists were a "little wild, but they had their serious side too. The real old timers," said Johnson, "like Sid Smith, Goldberg, Clare Briggs, DeBeck and Frank Willard (who drew the strip Johnson was to take over, 'Moon Mullins,' would cut loose and have their fun, then creep back to the drawing boards and do their wonderful cartoons."

Frederick Burr Opper, original drawing of Happy Hooligan, **$200.** Reprinted with special permission of King Features Syndicate, Inc.

73

Tex Blaisdell, sketch of Harold Gray's Little Orphan Annie and Sandy, **$75.** Reprinted by permission: Tribune Media Services.

Fontaine Fox, **$125.**

Edwina Dumm, original drawing of Tippie, **$30.**

Al Smith, original drawing of Captain Bud Fisher's characters Mutt and Jeff, **$65.**

Sidney Smith, original drawing of Andy Gump, **$200.**

Walt Hoban, original drawing of Jerry, from his strip "Jerry on the Job," **$150.** Reprinted with special permission of King Features Syndicate, Inc.

E.C. Segar, original drawing of Popeye, from his strip, "Thimble Theatre," **$400.** Reprinted with special permission of King Features Syndicate, Inc.

Billy DeBeck, original drawing of Barney Google, **$125.** Reprinted with special permission of King Features Syndicate, Inc.

Otto Soglow, self-portrait and sketch of The Little King, **$175.** Reprinted with special permission of King Features Syndicate, Inc.

Milt Gross, **$150.**

Bill Holman, **$40.**

Cliff Sterrett, **$150.**

Humorous strips continued to be popular throughout the late 1920s, but after the Depression, adventure stories began to dominate the comic sections and lasted many years. The adventure strip had appeared before this time, but it did not become established until the early 1930s with the publication of Nowland and Calkin's "Buck Rogers," and Harold Foster's "Tarzan." These stories changed the comics artistically, moving them away from caricatures and free-flowing style, and also transformed them from a disconnected series of gags to a continuing story. In many ways these changes paralleled developments occurring at the time in motion pictures, as the silent comedy began to lose its popularity to serials and other dramatic films.

Although the earliest adventure comics, such as "Tarzan" and "Buck Rogers," were based upon already existing novels and serializations, many new and original characters were introduced in the early thirties in an effort to capitalize on their success. The first originally inspired adventure comic was the work of Chester Gould, whose creation, "Dick Tracy," first appeared in 1931. For ten years prior to Tracy, Gould worked for several Chicago newspapers, trying desperately to sell his ideas for strips to the Chicago Tribune-New York Daily News Syndicate. Finally, Captain Joseph Medill Patterson of the Syndicate accepted Gould's idea for a strip entitled, "Plainclothes Tracy," and suggested that Tracy's name be changed to "Dick," a popular slang expression for detectives. Soon after Tracy made his debut, he became a cult figure of Prohibition America, and through the years he has changed very little, despite facing an ongoing barrage of villains who are continually added to

Chester Gould, original drawing of Dick Tracy, **$75.** Reprinted with permission: Tribune Media Services.

John Cullen Murphy, original drawing of Harold Foster's Prince Valiant, **$15.** Reprinted with special permission of King Features Syndicate, Inc.

Zack Mosley, original drawing of Smilin' Jack, **$35.**

FOR NEWTON LANE
— ALL THE BEST
FROM
MANDRAKE
THE MAGICIAN,
LOTHAR and
FRED
FREDERICKS

Fred Fredericks, original drawing of Lee Falk's and Phil Davis' Mandrake the Magician, **$45.** Reprinted with special permission of King Features Syndicate, Inc.

the strip's "Rogue's Gallery." Gould retired in 1977 and died in 1985, but Tracy agelessly continues in the hands of writer Max Collins and political cartoonist Dick Locher.

After the appearance of Dick Tracy, many other heroic characters were created, including Alex Raymond's "Jungle Jim" and "Flash Gordon"; Lee Falk's "Mandrake the Magician" and "The Phantom"; Milton Caniff's celebrated "Terry and the Pirates"; and Hal Foster's "Prince Valiant." Original strips from these artists can be very valuable today. A Hal Foster "Prince Valiant" original was sold for over $5,000, while an unusual 1941 "Terry and the Pirates" original by Caniff brought over $2,500 at auction. Original sketches of characters by these artists are in great demand, especially

since more time and work are involved in sketching them than a quick sketch of Krazy Kat. As a result, it is much harder to obtain original art from adventure strip cartoonists than from those who make comic drawings.

The broadening of the comic form also created opportunities for women cartoonists. This is not to say that women cartoonists could not function as excellent humorists, as several gifted cartoonists of the early period were women such as Edwina Dumm. Yet, newspaper publishers were more willing to employ women who produced adventure stories or serials, and the late 1930s and early 1940s saw a tremendous increase in the number of women cartoonists. Serial (or "soap opera") strips first appeared in the early thirties, with perhaps the most

Hi, Sig —
All Bestest
from Flash
and [signature: Dan Barry]
May '84
Sarasota, Fla.

Dan Barry, current Flash Gordon artist, self-portrait signed, **$15.**

significant being Martha Orr's "Apple Mary," (later changed to "Mary Worth"). The women cartoonists also produced some refreshingly different adventure strips as well, such as Dale Messick's "Brenda Starr." Today, of course, a woman cartoonist is not unusual in any comic strip genre and two of today's most respected humorists are cartoonists Lynn Johnston and Cathy Guisewite.

During World War II years, many comic strips dealt with war themes, several of which lost their popularity after the war was over. Nevertheless, many fine strips appeared during this period, including "Private Breger," by Dave Breger and Milton Caniff's "Steve Canyon," although this strip was updated to include the cold war. As might be expected during wartime, humorous material was temporarily set aside in favor of patriotic themes.

Humor, however, returned to the scene in a big way with the advent of the 1950s.

Adventure comics, so popular in the thirties and forties, experienced a declining readership in the 1950s because many important cartoonists died or entered into retirement, often leaving less talented cartoonists to carry on with their strips. A more important reason, however, was that humorous themes reappeared to dominate the comics. These new strips differed markedly from those of the twenties, and many contained philosophical and social commentary as well as humor. Walt Kelly's "Pogo" (1948) is an excellent example of this type of humorous strip, and it received tremendous critical acclaim. Kelly learned his trade working for the Walt Disney studios, and experimented with another strip before beginning

81

work on "Pogo." The strip featured a group of swamp animals, a good deal of introspective humor, and examined current political and social issues. Kelly died in the early 1970s. His strips, however, have remained very popular, especially among collectors, who have paid exorbitant prices for them. Kelly also did twenty-eight Pogo books for Simon and Schuster, and the original cover art has become very valuable. It currently sells for around $5,000.

The 1950s also witnessed the birth of several strips that have since become classics. Mort Walker's "Beetle Bailey," Hank Ketcham's "Dennis the Menace," and Johnny Hart's "B.C." all made their debut in the 1950s, although the most famous was Charles Schulz' classic "Peanuts."

Schulz polished his artistic skill through a correspondence course offered by Art Instruction, Inc., and spent time lettering cartoons for a religious publication before he created a strip called "Li'l Folks." After several unsuccessful attempts at selling the strip to the various newspaper syndicates, it was finally accepted by United Features in 1950. The syndicate, however, changed the name of the strip to "Peanuts."

Through the years "Peanuts" has been amazingly successful, spawning feature films, television specials, and numerous collections of strips. Schulz has exercised creative control over many of these projects, and still takes the time to do all of the work on his strips, including the lettering. His originals usually sell for $200 to $500, and are relatively rare, since many of his earlier strips were given away.

Dale Messick, original drawing of Brenda Starr, **$20.** Reprinted with permission: Tribune Media Services.

Hank Ketcham, original drawing of Dennis the Menace, **$40.** ©Hank Ketcham, 1985.

Mort Walker, original drawing of Beetle Bailey, **$25.** Reprinted with special permission of King Features Syndicate, Inc.

Irwin Hasen, original drawing of Dondi, **$15.** Reprinted with permission: Tribune Media Services.

Another popular strip that has survived admirably through the years, and still retains much of its original charm and humor, is Hank Ketcham's "Dennis the Menace." Dennis has been five years old since his birth on March 12, 1951, but Ketcham has prevented the strip from becoming stale with his superior graphic skill and good taste in humor. Ketcham frequently says that since a reader will pay attention to the strip only for a few seconds, "I'd better not have the panel confusing. I'd better have the line just right, the graphics just right."

Despite the many new features added to the comics during the 1950s, overall creativity declined and many newspaper syndicators faced economic disaster. Very few new strips were syndicated through the fifties and sixties, and by 1975, *Editor and Publisher* magazine revealed that only 200 strips were in nationwide syndication, an all-time low. Several reasons have been offered to explain this situation. The majority of established cartoonists were in their 60s and 70s at the time, and their deaths or retirement left a void that the syndicates were unwilling to fill with younger, sometimes unconventional, artists. There were many quality strips produced during the 1960s and early 1970s, including "The Wizard of Id," by Brant Parker and Johnny Hart, and Dik Browne's "Hagar the Horrible." But fewer people were reading the comics, and this spelled trouble both for newspapers (historically, the comics have been the most popular section of the newspaper) and for the cartooning industry.

Alex Kotzky, original sketch of two of the girls from "Apartment 3-G," **$15.** By permission of News America Syndicate.

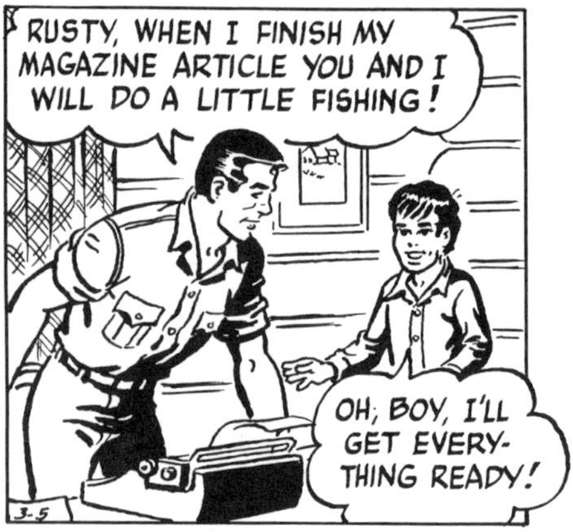
RUSTY, WHEN I FINISH MY MAGAZINE ARTICLE YOU AND I WILL DO A LITTLE FISHING!
OH, BOY, I'LL GET EVERY-THING READY!
3-5

"Mark Trail," original strip by Ed Dodd and Jack Elrod, inscribed to the author by the latter, **$70.** By permission of News America Syndicate.

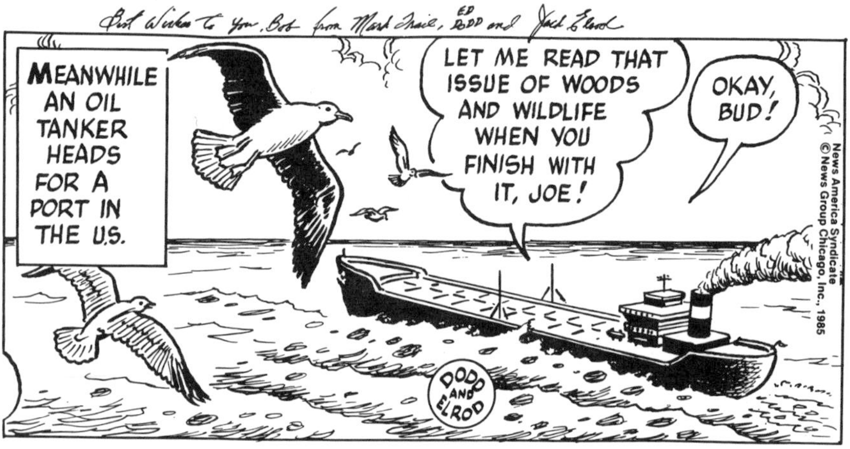
Best Wishes to you, Bob from Mark Trail, Ed Dodd and Jack Elrod
MEANWHILE AN OIL TANKER HEADS FOR A PORT IN THE U.S.
LET ME READ THAT ISSUE OF WOODS AND WILDLIFE WHEN YOU FINISH WITH IT, JOE!
OKAY, BUD!
News America Syndicate
© News Group Chicago, Inc., 1985
DODD AND ELROD

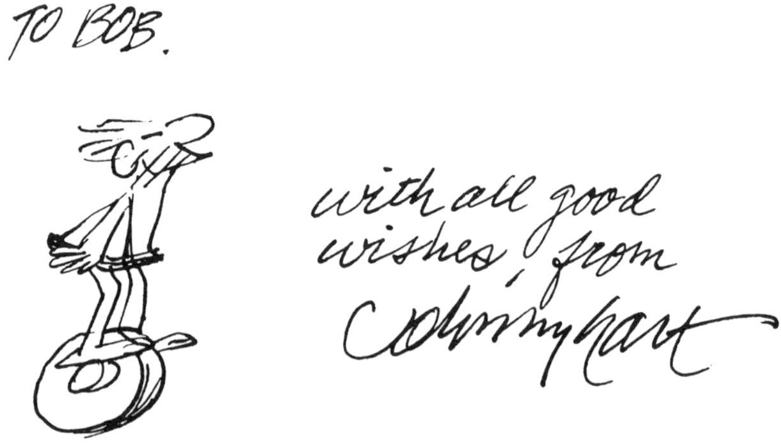
TO BOB.
with all good wishes, from
Johnny Hart

Johnny Hart, original drawing of B.C., **$15.** By permission of Johnny Hart and News America Syndicate.

To cousin Bob Bennett
Goodest wishes from Ol' Snuffy
& Fred Lasswell

3/24/81

Fred Lasswell, original drawing of Snuffy Smith, **$10.** Reprinted with special permission of King Features Syndicate, Inc.

Recently, the comics have once again experienced a new wave of popularity. Younger cartoonists have provided the medium with new conventions and new styles, and fresh and different strips are all over the comic page. The newer cartoonists have also brought an increased level of maturity to the cartooning arts. Political satire and adult situations are prominent in strips such as Trudeau's "Doonesbury," and Breathed's "Bloom County," strips also known for their oftentimes decadent humor. Growing families and their problems are also presented in today's strips. Issues relating to divorce and other marital problems are common material today, whereas mentioning these issues in an earlier strip would have been unheard of.

Ted Key, original drawing of Hazel, **$15.** Reprinted with special permission of King Features Syndicate, Inc.

Dik Browne, original drawing of Hagar the Horrible, **$25.** Reprinted with special permission of King Features Syndicate, Inc.

Berke Breathed, original drawing of Opus, from his strip "Bloom County," **$15.** ©1986 Washington Post Writers Group. Reprinted with permission.

FOR BRENDA

WHOOPS!
SORRY I MISSED YOUR BIRTHDAY!
— I WAS TIED UP!
JOHN CALDWELL

John Caldwell, self-portrait, **$10**.

Reg Smythe, original drawing of Andy Capp, **$15.** By permission of News America Syndicate.

Bill Hoest, original drawing of Leroy Lockhorn, **$10.** Reprinted with special permission of King Features Syndicate, Inc.

A recent trend in the comics is the one-panel gag cartoons containing visual puns and bizarre humor. The most popular of these has been Gary Larson's "The Far Side," and Kevin Pope's fine "Inside Out." In many ways, these cartoons hark back to the earliest days of the comics where off-the-wall gags were the rule of the day, notably in cartoons by Rube Goldberg in the twenties and Bill Holman in the thirties and forties.

There is an amazing variety in the pages of current comic sections, and original sketches and strips may be requested from a host of talented artists. Some of the most popular cartoonists include Jim Davis, who draws both "Garfield" and "U.S. Acres," Gary Trudeau and Berke Breathed, women cartoonists Lynn Johnston and Cathy Guisewite, and Gary Larson of "The Far Side." Trudeau and Davis are not very receptive to requests for original art, but with so many artists to choose from, you should still be able to assemble a fine collection.

BIZARRO.

Dan Piraro original sketch, **$10.**

Comic strips provide a rich source of material for collectors, and building an extensive collection of original strips and sketches takes a lot of time and initiative. But, if you are interested in acquiring a broader collection of comic art, you might consider adding original comic book art to your collection. Or, you may even wish to specialize in this field. Although comic book art is generally less valuable than comic strip art, there is a wealth of interesting material available that would enhance any collection of cartoon art.

The comic book, like comic strips, also originated in Germany. Wilhelm Busch's creations appeared in comic book form, and other German artists' creations soon followed. In America, several popular comic strips, such as "Bringing Up Father" and "Little Orphan Annie," were reprinted in book form, but the first comic book with original material was *New Fun* in 1934. Although *New Fun* consisted of mostly humorous material, the majority of the early comic books contained

adventure stories. Yet, by the end of the 1930s, no character of any significance had emerged from comic books. That is, until Superman burst onto the scene in the June 1938 issue of *Action Comics*.

Superman was created by two 17-year-olds, Jerry Siegel and Joe Shuster and immediately became a huge popular success. In the process, Superman also made the comic book successful, and generated a wave of imitations, such as Bob Kane's Batman, and C. C. Beck's Captain Marvel. Eventually Superman also became a newspaper strip, first drawn by Siegel and Shuster, and then by Wayne Boring. Boring is perhaps the finest artist associated with the character; the work of Siegel and Shuster was crude and amateurish, and publishers refused to reprint their work for many years. Nevertheless, their original strips and artwork are very valuable, and would make an excellent investment if located. Superman remains

S.M. "Jerry" Iger, original sketches of (A) Pee Wee and (B) Bobby, two of the earliest comic book characters, **$35.**

one of the most popular and well-known comic heroes ever created, and any original art connected with the character brings a high price. Original strips and book art are scarce, but original sketches by Boring and the character's current artists, Curt Swan and Murphey Anderson, can be obtained rather easily by mail.

Superman's popularity established the comic book as an important force in the world of cartoon art. New publishers included D. C. (now National Periodical Publications) and Marvel. Over the years, these two publishers have produced an amazing array of "super-heroes," including Stan Lee's

Spiderman, Robert Howard's Conan the Barbarian, and Kirby and Simon's Captain America, all of which have ventured beyond the comic book and become either newspaper strips, animated cartoons, or Hollywood films. Hollywood has drawn on several comic book characters for feature films and television series, and doubtless more will follow in the future. Through film and television appearances, comic book characters have reached a much wider audience, but, as a result, the popularity of the comic book has declined. Comic books were once available at nearly every newsstand or grocery store, but they are a little harder to find now.

Super-heroes have long been the mainstay of comic books, but popular comics have also featured a variety of other characters. Only a few comic strip characters have made successful sojourns to comic books, but animated characters have fared considerably better. Disney characters have enjoyed a great deal of popularity in the pages of comic books, and many fine artists have contributed to their success. There have been scores of animated characters, from Bugs Bunny to Casper the Friendly Ghost, who have appeared in comic books, but the work of the Disney artists has been unsurpassed. In particular, the work of Carl Barks has been most exceptional, and his originals are highly valued.

Historically, comic books have been largely imitative of newspaper cartoons. Adventure stories started in the newspaper, and aside from creating several outstanding super-hero characters, comic book adventures have not matched the quality or the inventiveness present in the newspaper strip. Nevertheless, comic books have ventured into areas where the newspaper strip, due to its wide readership, could never go.

One of the earliest examples of creativity and daring in the comic book can be found in the gory comics produced by William Gaines in the 1950s. Gaines' E. C. Comics have been criticized for their gruesome displays of violence and bloodshed, but the art and the storylines in these publications were often of very high quality. The criticism leveled at E. C. for their gory graphics and mature themes took on an even greater significance as the decade unfolded. In 1954, after the publication of Dr. Frederick Wertham's anti-comic book essay, *Seduction of the Innocent,* the U.S. Senate held

Wayne Boring, original drawing of Superman, **$30.** ©National Periodical Publications.

Ernie Chan, original drawing of Conan the Barbarian, **$25.** ©Marvel Comics Group.

93

hearings to determine whether or not to censor the comics. Fearing censorship, comic book publishers established the Comics Code Authority, a self-regulating body that operates in much the same way as did the motion picture code. In addition to regulating sex and violence in the comics, however, the code also exercises influence over the presentation of social and political ideas. Part of its general standards, for instance, state that "policemen, judges, government officials and other respected institutions shall not be presented in such a way as to create disrespect for established authority." The Comics Code is so far-reaching that it goes beyond what would be constitutionally acceptable if regulated by the government.

Due to the presence of the Comics Code, many of the most creative comic book artists of the fifties and sixties were forced "underground." Although these artists were still troubled by lawsuits and censorship (much of their work bordered on pornography), they experienced a boom in popularity in the anti-establishment 1960s.

The most important and unconventional underground cartoonist is Robert Crumb. Crumb created the characters Fritz the Cat and Mr. Natural while pioneering an off-beat artistic style. His work, and the work of other underground artists, such as Gilbert Shelton (creator of The Fabulous Furry Freak Brothers), dealt heavily with sex, drugs, and violence, but in many ways also returned to the free-flowing gag cartoons of the 1920s inspired by the work of Herriman, Segar, and others.

Everett Raymond Kinstler, original drawing of Zorro, as he appeared in comic books, **$15.**

"Henry," original strip by John Liney, who took over the daily panel from creator Carl Anderson, **$70.** Reprinted with special permission of King Features Syndicate, Inc.

The work of the underground cartoonists is also very popular with collectors of original art. It is unique, colorful, and highly unusual, although difficult to locate. Crumb is a recluse, and the whereabouts of other underground practitioners are unknown. But if you are interested in building an extensive collection of original comic book art, you should endeavor to locate this material as it will truly broaden your collection.

RELENTLESSLY, OVER MILES OF WINDING ROAD, JINGLES PURSUES THE FLEEING KIDNAPPER.

Our examination of the history of the comic strip has omitted many classic strips and fine comic artists, but this does not mean that material other than what we have mentioned is not worthy of collecting. Almost any original strip or sketch is worth obtaining, if the price is reasonable. Keep in mind, however, that the most valuable strips are those that possess the greatest historical or artistic significance. Nevertheless, a collection that includes a wide variety of minor strips, such as a collection featuring examples from several different comic strip genres, may also become very valuable. And if a certain strip has sentimental value to you, don't shy way from purchasing it just because it may never be very valuable. After all, in collecting virtually anything, a primary concern should be having fun.

We have not discussed several other strips that make excellent investments. Cartoonists producing strips in various

WOW! I'M GOING TOO FAST FOR THIS HAIRPIN... I'LL NEVER MAKE IT!

foreign countries have created many wonderful originals, and only a small portion of their work has been syndicated in the United States. Material from foreign cartoonists is difficult to obtain, and is usually available in the United States only at auctions or comic conventions. If possible, you may

"Smoky Dawson," original strip by Albert DeVine, **$50.**

wish to attend European comic conventions and art shows to improve your chances of obtaining this material. A very thorough volume, which provides an excellent idea of what is available from both American and foreign cartoonists, is Maurice Horn's *The World Encyclopedia of Comics* (1979), which may be found in your local library. This book is also an excellent reference source, of use in identifying certain cartoons and artists, and in determining whether the work possesses any historical or artistic importance.

Original comic art is available in two basic forms. Original strips, comic book art, or comic book covers, comprise one available form, and original sketches and drawings (those made expressly for collectors) constitutes the other. Generally, the original artwork that goes into the production of a newspaper strip or comic book is the more valuable. A drawing made for a collector has considerably less value, unless it is a very elaborate work of higher quality than comic strip or comic book art.

Original strips are usually the most valuable as well as the most popular material. Prices can range from $50 for an insignificant daily strip, to $5,000 or more for a very rare strip in great demand.

Dear Bob —
Sure, sounds fine,
Good luck with the book.

JERRY DUMAS

Jerry Dumas, cartoonist of "Sam and Silo," sketch of a cat, **$10.**

A dog.
↓ (I just
felt like
doodling)

Jim
Meddick

Jim Meddick, cartoonist of "Robot Man," sketch of a dog, **$10.**

From the earliest days of the cartoon, original strips were published in color, and, of course, all things being equal, a color (Sunday) strip is worth more than a black and white strip. Original strips are also much larger than they appear in newspapers, and usually meaure about 6″ to 7″ by 15″ to 20″. Before being placed under the camera and reduced for newspaper publication, some strips have a rather crude appearance (most contain blue pencil lines or other pencil work on the front and back) while others reveal great depth and beauty that is not always apparent when the strip is printed. These factors, of course, will shape the price of an original as will rarity, demand, and historical and artistic importance.

Many original strips contain pencil markings that are of use to the artist in drawing the characters. Other artists prefer another technique and they sketch a preliminary strip. Preliminary strips are available from few artists as most of them are probably discarded. Usually done in heavy pencil, they are cheaper than original, finished, strips, and you may be interested in them if you have limited funds to spend on your collection.

Virginia and George Smith, original drawing of their son, **$10.** By permission of Virginia and George Smith.

Comic book art is similar to strip art, although it is almost always in color. Comic book art may be sold by the page or by the panel, depending upon how the artist prepared the work, and originals are larger than they appear when published. Comic book covers are generally more valuable than the inside artwork and can be worth as much as $5,000, or more. The most valuable are Disney covers, especially those of Carl Barks, and the covers for Walt Kelly's Pogo collections.

The easiest originals to obtain are sketches and drawings made for collectors. These are either obtained in person, usually on album pages, or by mail on index cards or sheets of art paper. Occasionally, paintings or watercolors of certain characters become available, and these can be worth more than original strips or comic book art if they are of substantial quality. The average original drawings or sketches are worth about $5 to $25 each, although those from deceased cartoonists might sell for as much as $500 or more. Since they can be obtained by writing to cartoonists,

a valuable collection of original sketches may be built for the cost of postage.

When writing to cartoonists through the mail, and in collecting other original comic art, you risk the problem of unauthentic artwork prepared by the cartoonist's assistant, or you may receive printed copies of the artist's work. Printed artwork is usually sent out on large cards or sheets of art paper, and sometimes bears an authentic ink signature of the cartoonist. These items are prepared specifically for the purpose of answering the many requests for drawings that a cartoonist receives. They do not, however, pose a problem if you learn how to tell printer's ink, which is dull and lacking in color variation, to artist's ink.

Printed facsimilies of artwork should not be confused with lithographs. Lithographs of artwork are not original, but they are limited edition prints that may have considerably more value than the printed artwork sent to collectors. If you are interested in collecting signed lithographs rather than original art, an excellent selection of

Bud Blake, original drawing of Tiger, **$15.**
Reprinted with special permission of King
Features Syndicate, Inc.

contemporary material is available from Stabur Enterprises, 23301 Meadow Park, Detroit, Michigan 48239.

Many of the famous older cartoonists—and increasingly, many of the younger ones as well—have been known to hire assistants to "ghost" their strips. Hank Ketcham of "Dennis the Menace" employs two assistants to produce the Sunday edition of his strip. This fact raises quite a few problems for collectors of comic art. If a cartoonist has achieved great fame, or if he or she has a distinctive artistic style, their work will be worth more than the work of an assistant. The collector must determine whether the strip was drawn by the cartoonist whose signature appears on the strip or his assistants. There are a couple of ways to help solve this problem. First of all, when buying cartoon art advertised as the work of a certain person, proceed with caution. Be wary of "expert" opinions and do your own investigating. This should include finding all the information you can about the artist and the strip. There are several books detailing the history of the comics in the library to assist you in this task. Reading a few of the current comic publications should also prove helpful, especially in regard to more contemporary artists.

When collecting original sketches through the mail you must also be on the lookout for sketches made by assistants. When writing, try to impress upon the cartoonist that you are a serious collector of authentic and original material. More often than not, if your request is also polite, this approach will prove successful. If you suspect that you have received work of an assistant, you might try comparing the signature on the drawing to the authentic signature of the cartoonist (usually the signature on a strip appearing in the newspaper is an authentic example). Aside from this, there is not too much you can do to authenticate the sketch unless the cartoonist who purportedly drew it has such a distinctive style that it is not capable of being duplicated. The presence of non-original or unauthentic artwork may make collecting comic art more complex, but it should not prove impossible or affect your enjoyment of the hobby to a great degree. Acquiring original comic art is relatively free of great difficulty, especially if you are a careful and somewhat skeptical collector.

Collecting comic art is a hobby growing in importance and popularity. The comics are experiencing a new wave of success and original artwork is continually being added to museums and fine art galleries, increasing its value dramatically. The years ahead are sure to offer knowledgeable collectors exciting investment opportunites, and a great deal of enjoyment.

Bil Keane, original drawing of Billy from "Family Circus," **$10.** ©1986 Cowles Syndicate, Inc.

4 Newspaper and Magazine Cartoons

Patrick Oliphant, sketch of Jimmy Carter, $20.

The newspaper and magazine cartoon world differs considerably from that of the comic strip or animated film. Comic cartoons are among the most widely read features in hundreds of different publications, and the famous characters and heroes of the comics have achieved enormous popular success. The political and editorial cartoon, on the other hand, appeals only to a very small segment of the public, and a magazine panel is normally viewed only by the readership of the publication in question. Popular characters are absent from editorial or magazine cartoons, unless, of course, one wants to include prominent figures in this category.

This does not mean that newspaper and magazine cartoons are without importance. Political cartoons are among the wittiest of all intellectual statements, and the bite of today's top political cartoonists is felt with an increasing level of influence. In addition, many of the finest artists working within the cartooning arts are associated with the editorial or political cartoon, or with prestigious publications such as *The New Yorker*.

The high level of artistic skill and the intellectual brilliance of many newspaper and magazine cartoons have also generated interest among cartoon art collectors. Original political cartoons have increasing historical significance, and are widely sought after by art collectors, historians, and collectors of documents and manuscripts. The work of such noted magazine cartoonists as Hirshfield, Charles Addams or Edward Koren, has brought high prices at auctions of original art. Hirschfield's original caricatures, for instance, sell for $500 to $1,000 each.

Satirical drawings and caricatures of royalty or famous political figures became popular in Europe during the eighteenth century, but the first real political cartoonist was Thomas Nast. Nast was born in Bavaria in 1840, and immigrated to America in 1846. During the 1860s, he started drawing for *Harper's Weekly* and other journals, and after serving in the Civil War, used his cartoons to attack the political corruption of the 1860s and 1870s. During this time, he also created the Republican elephant and the Democratic jackass. His most famous cartoons were those attacking the corrupt Boss Tweed and the Tammany Hall political machine that ruled New York City during the 1870s. Nast's work tripled the circulation of *Harper's,* and eventually helped put an end to Tweed's activities. Before his career was over, Nast was appointed American consul to Guayaquil in Ecuador where he died in 1902.

Nast's original cartoons are very rare, and bring excessive prices at auctions. His most valuable cartoons are those dealing with Tammany Hall or the trusts, or other themes attacking corrupt activities of politicians or businessmen. His original sketches are also available, and are usually priced around $75 to $100. A signature of Nast is worth about $50.

Besides Nast, there have been hundreds of political cartoonists through the years who have produced many wonderful panels worthy of collecting. Another great political cartoonist of the early period of the editorial cartoon was Frederick Opper, who drew the comic strip "Happy Hooligan." Opper was a gifted artist, and his satirizations of oil tycoons and politicians from Bryan to Hoover were as familiar to the public as his comic characters.

During the 1940s and 1950s, two other distinguished political cartoonists, Herbert Block (known as "Herblock") and Bill Mauldin appeared on the cartoon scene. Mauldin was the creator of the definitive World War II soldiers, Willie and Joe,

Thomas Nast, original self-portrait signed, **$150.**

Ronald Reagan, as seen by some of America's finest political cartoonists.

Kate Salley Palmer, **$10.**

Tony Auth, **$15.**

Dick Locher, **$15.**

Bob Rich, **$10.**

and Block's witty panels have established the standard format and appearance of today's political cartoon. They have been joined by dozens of fine artists who have set new standards for humor and inventiveness, including Patrick Oliphant, Jeff MacNelly, Draper Hill, John Trever, Tony Auth, Don Wright, and Jim Borgman, to name a few. Original cartoons and sketches by these artists will make fine additions to your collection. Most can be written to in care of their newspapers, and many can be persuaded to make sketches of current political leaders. In this chapter, you'll see how some of today's political cartoonists view Ronald Reagan. And for a look at how Reagan views himself, see chapter 6.

Draper Hill, **$15.**

Editorial cartoonist Ken Alexander, self-portrait, **$5.**

Jim Borgman, self-portrait, **$5.**

Raymond Osrin, self-portrait, **$5.**

To Sig Armitage with best wishes,

Art Bimrose
Editorial Cartoonist
The Oregonian, Retired

5/84

Art Bimrose, self-portrait, **$5.**

Editorial cartoons are similar to political cartoons in many ways, except that they may deal more with current events and social issues rather than politics. There are several editorial panels and strips in the newspaper, including Jim Berry's "Berry's World" and Morrie Brickman's "The Small Society," as well as David Seavey's illustrations in *USA Today.* But the most famous of all editorial cartoonists is the award-winning artist, Jules Feiffer.

Feiffer was born in 1929 in the Bronx, and after high school, he began his career by working as an assistant on a comic strip and later at an animation studio. In 1956, he began working for the *Village Voice,* doing a weekly strip he called "Feiffer." The strip features a sparse drawing style, and a healthy dose of irony and wit. Through the years, many other cartoonists,

For Fred Bennetto with best wishes.

Jim Berry

Jim Berry of "Berry's World," self-portrait, **$10.**

David Seavey, *USA Today* editorial cartoonist, self-portrait, **$10.**

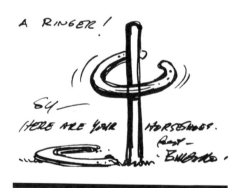

Sports cartoonist Bill Gallo, sketch of a horseshoe game, **$10.**

whether working on political cartoons or in the comic pages, have tried to imitate Feiffer's work, but his original style still has a uniqueness all its own.

Sports cartoons may also be found in your daily newspaper, and there are a few nationally syndicated sports cartoonists who can be written to for original cartoons and drawings. Bill Whitehead's panel, "Sidelines," is probably the most famous sports panel, but the work of noted cartoonists Bill Gallo and Phil Bissell has also attracted some nationwide attention.

There is an amazing range among the cartoons that appear in newspapers and other publications. Almost every taste is catered to, from the witty and distinguished cartoons of *The New Yorker* to the oftentimes crude (but nevertheless funny) cartoons of *Mad, Playboy,* or *National Lampoon.* In between, there are a host of other publications that regularly feature cartoons dealing with humorous themes, politics, or current events. Most of today's top magazine cartoonists contribute to several publications, and their work is available to many thousands of readers.

The New Yorker magazine has featured many of the best magazine cartoons by some of the most renowned of all cartoonists. Artists such as Charles Addams, William Hamilton, Eldon Dedini, Robert Weber, Everett Opie, Roz Chast, and many others have been associated with *The New Yorker,* and much of their best work has been assembled in the recent book *The New Yorker Cartoon Collection.* Original cartoons from these artists usually sell for $50 to $100 or more, depending upon the cartoonist and the

Sports cartoonist Phil Bissell, self-portrait, **$10.**

The New Yorker cartoonist William Hamilton, **$10.**

Charles Addams, original drawing of Uncle Fester, **$20.**

Robert Weber, **$10.**

Paul Rigby, $5.

Jim Thompson, $5.

Yours with enthusiasm !
and Kewpish love
for all children
and child-lovers,

Rose O'Neill

Rose O'Neill, creator of the Kewpie Doll, signature, **$35.**

To BOB BENNETT
WITH BEST WISHES

Orlando Busino, **$10**

age of the cartoon. Some of the more famous cartoons might fetch a higher price. Opie's work usually brings $150 to $200 per cartoon. Most of the above artists are also willing to make sketches for collectors, and can be written to in care of the publication.

There are several publications that publish the work of *The New Yorker* regulars and other magazines. Among these publications are *TV Guide* and *Good Housekeeping. TV Guide* publishes the work of many major cartoonists when their cartoons deal with the subject of television. Those who have contributed to *TV Guide* include Lou Myers, Chon Day, Mort Gerberg, and Rowland Wilson.

Good Housekeeping magazine, along with many other women's magazines, was among the first to include cartoons in its pages. In the 1910s, *Good Housekeeping* became the first major publication to publish Rose O'Neill's famous Kewpie doll drawings. Public reaction to O'Neill's work was astonishing, and this caused O'Neill to syndicate a Sunday comic strip featuring her creations. Today, *Good Housekeeping* sets few trends with its cartoons, but a few talented artists, such as Chon Day and Orlando Busino, regularly contribute lighthearted and amusing panels for its readers.

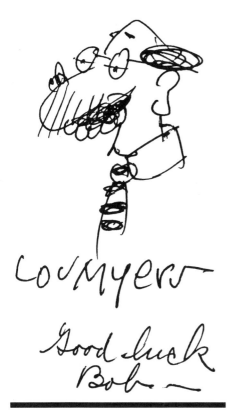

Boris Drucker, self-portrait, **$10.**

Lou Myers, **$10.**

A great virtue of the magazine cartoon is that it is almost completely without a format. Virtually anything imaginable can be presented in a magazine cartoon, as long as it fits into a panel. Thus far, we have discussed only the more or less traditional magazine cartoon, featured not only in *The New Yorker, TV Guide* or *Good Housekeeping,* but also in such publications as *Puck, Judge, Life, Harper's,* or *Ladies' Home Journal.* But dozens of other magazines, such as *Mad, National Lampoon,* or *Playboy,* have popularized a very different approach to the magazine cartoon.

Chon Day, original drawing of Brother Sebastian, **$15.**

Mad magazine cartoonist Sergio Aragones, $15.

Mad magazine was created in 1952 by illustrator Harvey Kurtzman. At the time Kurtzman was employed by William Gaines' E. C. Comics, and had worked on some of the horror publications that helped bring about the self-censorship of the comic industry. *Mad* became an instant success, and also served to revolutionize comic books and magazine cartoons. Although Kurtzman left *Mad* in 1955, he was responsible for many innovations, including satirizations and parodies of the comics, movies, television, and advertising. *Mad* caused a sensation after its release, and remained much the same throughout the 1950s and 1960s, but its appeal has almost always been limited to younger teenagers. Nevertheless, *Mad's* publishers have assembled a fine and talented group of cartoonists who have kept its humor fresh and spontaneous. The most famous cartoonists to contribute to *Mad* have probably been Don Martin and Sergio Aragones, but the work of dozens of other fine artists, including Jack Davis, Mort Drucker, Dave Berg, and Bob Clarke (who was responsible for *Mad's* many wonderful parodies of the comics), continue to grace its pages.

Billed as the "humor magazine for adults," many of the cartoons published in *National Lampoon* are simply more mature and bizarre renditions of the kind of material available in *Mad* or *The New Yorker.* Several distinguished cartoonists draw panels for *National Lampoon,* including Sam Gross, Robert Mankoff, Thomas Cheney, and Gahan Wilson, and these cartoons rival *The New Yorker's* in wit and inventiveness. Some of the *National Lampoon* artists also draw for *The New Yorker,* but the *Lampoon* offers these artists more freedom to deal with themes that *The New Yorker's* readers might find "tasteless." Certainly, much of the material in *National Lampoon* is not for the easily offended; sexual situations abound, and "sick" humor is the rule rather than the exception. But the creativity and artistic skill of many of the contributors to *National Lampoon* should not be overlooked.

Gordon" newspaper strips. *National Lampoon* does not, however, confine itself to parodies of comic strips, but has also introduced several original features, including Ron Barrett's "Politenessman" and B. K. Taylor's "Timberland Tales." The humor in these strips is off-the-wall to say the least, and many *Lampoon* artists are former "underground" cartoonists, a sure sign that they consider no subject matter off limits.

Cartoons that appear in *Playboy* magazine, contrary to public belief, do not always deal with the subject of sex. Sexual material, of course, is the chief preoccupation of *Playboy,* and some of the magazine's cartoonists, such as Christopher Browne (son of "Hagar the Horrible's" Dik Browne), John Dempsey, and Buck Brown, almost always draw sexually-oriented cartoons. But a large number of very distinguished cartoonists contribute to *Playboy,* and sex is not their exclusive subject. The work of renowned illustrators such as Shel Silverstein and

---

Don Martin, **$10.**

National Lampoon, like *Mad,* also offers parodies of the movies and the comics, but those in the *Lampoon* are much more subtle and sophisticated. An interesting fact is that many of the artists who work on these parodies for *National Lampoon* are older generation cartoonists who helped produce much of what is being parodied. These artists include Leslie Cabarga, a noted animator for the Max Fleischer Studios in the 1930s, and Russ Heath, a gifted comic book artist of the forties and fifties, who also assisted with both the "Terry and the Pirates" and "Flash

Mike Twohy, **$5.**

National Lampoon cartoonist Rick Geary, **$5.**

M.K. Brown, original drawing of Aunt Mary, **$10.**

Charles Rodrigues, original drawing of Deidre Callahan, **$10.**

Gahan Wilson, **$15.**

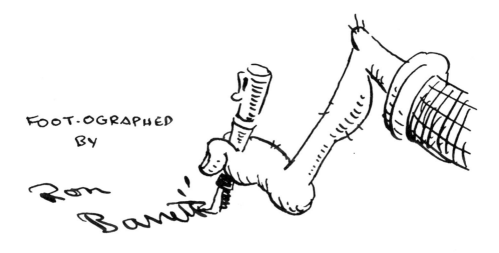

Ron Barrett, **$5.**

Playboy cartoonist John Dempsey, self-portrait, **$10.**

Bernard Kliban can regularly be found in *Playboy,* and cartoonists such as Eldon Dedini, Barsotti, Sidney Harris, Gahan Wilson, Charles Rodrigues, and Mort Gerberg have also produced fine artwork for the publication. *Playboy* has been one of the leading publishers of irreverent magazine cartoons in recent years, and has assembled one of the finest groups of artists currently involved in drawing cartoons.

Original *Playboy* art has been very popular among cartoon art collectors, as well as those interested in collecting magazine and other publication art. Most of *Playboy's* art is published in color, and color originals bring higher prices than black and white cartoons. Cartoonists whose work appears in *Playboy* may be addressed in care of the magazine, and in the past *Playboy* has been very good about forwarding mail to them.

We have covered many of the major publishers of magazine cartoons in this chapter, but there are many other past and present periodicals that we have failed to mention. In addition, hundreds of publications no longer in existence have published cartoons, and the originals may be available from dealers or auction houses. Besides the quality of an original cartoon, and the fame of the artist, the magazine in which the cartoon originally appeared is an important factor in determining value. A cartoon appearing in *The New Yorker* or *Playboy* is generally worth more than one appearing in *Good Housekeeping,* or an even smaller publication. When collecting contemporary originals, it is best to concentrate on the cartoons appearing in major publications, while collecting older material calls for a slightly different approach. Try to search out originals from some of the classic magazines of the past including *Life, Harper's,* or *The Saturday Evening Post,* and of course, older issues of *The New Yorker.*

Original cartoon by Roy Nixon, **$10.**

Original cartoon by G. Troop, **$10.**

"Well!! You finally made it! I got here early so I could just see how long you'd keep me waiting!!" Original cartoon by John F. Dunnett, **$10.**

"Gee, Dad, I didn't think Mommy was stronger than you, but I heard her say she can twist you around her little finger!" Original cartoon by Jeffry J. Monahan, **$15.**

If you decide to collect original cartoons from some of the older publications, it is a good idea to acquaint yourself with what is available by visiting a library. Most larger libraries keep a good supply of many of the classic magazines of the past, and, by leafing through a few of them, you may gain an insight into what is really valuable and worth collecting. Discover for yourself where your interests may lie. In perusing these publications, you will also learn to distinguish the magazine cartoon from illustration art, which is covered in the next chapter.

"YES DEAR — FIRST, YOU TAKE HIS NAME, THEN, YOU TAKE HIS HOUSE, HIS CAR, HIS BANK ACCOUNT, HIS INSURANCE AND ALL HIS SECURITIES!"

Original cartoon by Jack Flynn, $10.

Magazine cartoons are usually single panels with captions, although a few magazines publish cartoons that are similar in form to a newspaper comic strip. Illustration art, by contrast, is usually in the form of a watercolor or oil painting when featured in a magazine, but almost never in the form of a cartoon. The paintings of Norman Rockwell, which have graced the covers of *The Saturday Evening Post*, are examples of illustration art. A Rockwell painting may be easy to distinguish from a Charles Addams cartoon, but in some cases, the differences between cartoons and illustrations may be more difficult to discern. The work of Al Hirschfield, the *New York Times* caricaturist, can be placed into both categories, as might also be covers for *The New Yorker* drawn by Edward Koren. There are dozens of artists who have produced both illustrations and cartoons, including the great A. B. Frost, both a noted cartoonist and the illustrator of the famous *Uncle Remus* stories. But the primary difference between the two is that an illustration is used to accompany text when found in a magazine, and is usually a painting. A cartoon is a feature unto itself with much simpler graphics.

Original magazine cartoons are not often found where comic or animation art is sold. The most distinguished, artistic, and classic magazine cartoons are found almost exclusively at auction, but also may be located for sale in paper collectible or antiques journals. Many sellers of old magazines frequently deal in original cartoons, and writing to some of the more established magazine dealers may put you in touch with quite a few sellers of cartoon art. Political cartoons also are sold by manuscript dealers, or sellers of autographs or historical documents. Some of these dealers will be listed in chapter 6.

Most original political or magazine cartoons measure about 8½″ by 11″, the standard size of drawing paper. A few others may range in size from roughly 5″ by 7″ to about 11″ by 14″. The great majority of originals are drawn with pen and ink, or charcoals, and rarely will an original be prepared in pencil. Color originals are much less common than those in black and white (since only a few publications have printed their cartoons in color), but, when they are available, they are most often produced with watercolors.

In assessing the value of political or magazine cartoons, there are several judgments involved. In regard to the political cartoon, the primary focus is the subject matter. The fame of the cartoonist and the age of the cartoon are important factors, but major historical events depicted in an original cartoon bring much higher prices than routine or unimportant happenings. The political leader pictured in a cartoon may also help to determine value. A panel roasting Richard Nixon will probably fetch a higher price than one featuring a more obscure politician.

Thomas Cheney, **$10.**

Graham Hunter, self-portrait, **$5.**

Jim Venable, self-portrait, **$10.**

Jim Ivey, self-portrait, **$5.**

Ed Arno, self-portrait, **$5.**

Fred Englehart, self-portrait, **$5.**

Two sketches made for a collector by cartoonist Smith, **$20.**

Among serious collectors, the work of Thomas Nast also possesses great value, especially his famous cartoons attacking the trusts or Tammany Hall. And, of course, a famous political cartoonist (such as Frederick Opper) will also command high prices for his work. But it is most important to remember that the historical value of a cartoon is an element in determining its monetary value.

We have mentioned the importance of which magazine publishes a cartoon in shaping its value. Other considerations involve the fame of the cartoonist, the elaboration of the cartoon, and humor, too, may be important in establishing value. A cartoon must be funny and we have included a few humorless cartoons in this chapter for reference.

Original sketches of both political and editorial cartoonists, or magazine cartoonists, are fairly easy to obtain, and are valued at $5 to $25, or even more if made by a deceased or very famous cartoonist.

When writing to political cartoonists, you should try to elicit sketches of famous political figures. Self-portraits or other sketches made by them have less value. Most of the time it is easy to persuade these artists to sketch a political figure, and occasionally they may even send you an original panel. As always, remember a polite and sincere letter usually will obtain the best response.

Magazine cartoonists rarely draw a specific character, and while this may seem to be a drawback, it can actually be very positive. A magazine cartoonist might make you a self-portrait, or draw an animal or humorous face. But there are a few magazine cartoonists who will take the time to draw something really innovative for you.

Every once in a while, a magazine artist will even create a special "gag" drawing just for you. It is generally not a good idea to ask the cartoonist to do something special, but if you write an interesting letter, your chances of obtaining a unique item are fairly good.

Political and magazine cartoons can make wonderful cartoon art collectibles, and are among the most interesting to collect. Although it is true that this field is not as glamorous as animation or the comics, it does offer many opportunities to obtain very interesting works of art at often reasonable prices. If you are at all interested in history, politics, sports, current events, or famous periodicals—as well as humor —then this area of the hobby just might appeal to you.

5 Illustration Art

Illustration art is more commonly perceived as a branch of fine art rather than cartoon art, but there are several reasons why cartoon art collectors also collect illustration art. There is often a fine line between illustrations and cartoons. The work of Dr. Seuss and other children's book illustrators is very similar to the style and graphics of comics or animated films. Magazine cartoons can be hard to distinguish from illustrations in many cases. There is also some crossover between cartoon and illustration art as several noted artists have worked in both mediums.

A major reason why illustration art is often closely connected to fine art is its high price. Original paintings, used as book or magazine illustrations, have sold for hundreds of thousands of dollars, well within the price range of pieces of fine art. Most major auction houses, when selling illustration art, feature it under "American paintings" or "19th century paintings," and hence, it is often grouped wih fine art rather than placed in its own category. Illustration art is by far the most expensive "cartoon" artwork to collect; prices for large oil or watercolor paintings begin around $5,000, and sketches or smaller paintings often start at prices exceeding $1,000. Nevertheless, there are bargains to be found in this

Arthur William Brown, **$35.**

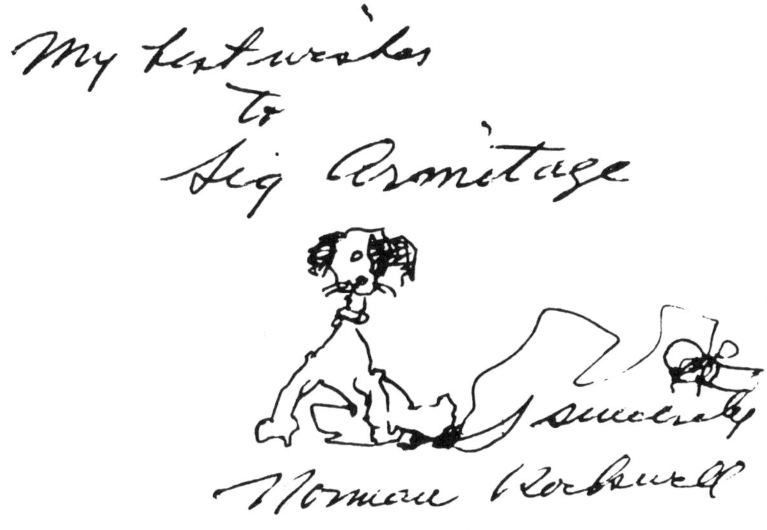
My best wishes
to
Sig Armitage
Sincerely
Norman Rockwell

Norman Rockwell, original drawing of a dog, **$55.**

field, and original sketches of illustrators may be obtained relatively inexpensively, either through sales or by writing to illustrators.

Among the most valuable pieces of illustration art are magazine illustrations. Many classic publications, such as *The Saturday Evening Post,* have included magnificent cover art, by artists as renowned as Norman Rockwell, Stevan Dohanos, Howard Chandler Christie, and Saul Tepper. Rockwell's paintings seldom sell for under $100,000, and one of his works, *The Homecoming,* brought $253,000 at auction in 1981. Dohanos, one of the first photorealists of illustration, is famous for some of the cover art he produced during the 1950s. His works are usually priced under $10,000 each, but his famous painting *Pete's Double Header,* a widely exhibited classic, recently sold for $18,000 at auction.

There are literally thousands of artists who have provided magazine illustrations that carry great value. *The Saturday Evening Post* is one of the most important sources, but dozens of other publications have also published famous works. Some of the most expensive magazine illustrations have appeared in periodicals as diverse as *The New Yorker, Harpers, The American Weekly,* or even *Esquire. Esquire* illustrations, in particular, have captured the fancy of many collectors, especially the drawings of women made by Vargas and Petty during the 1940s. An Alberto Vargas airbrush watercolor, made in 1940, recently sold for over $12,000 at an auction of illustration art. Rarely will high quality illustrations fall below $10,000 in price, and thus, illustration art is a field of collecting reserved for the fairly affluent collector.

Frederick Remington, western artist, **$100,**

Dr. Seuss, original drawing of The Cat in the Hat, **$75.** ©1985 Theodor Seuss Geisel.

Even advertisements or promotional artwork published in classic publications have achieved great value. Paintings and other illustrations used in advertisements of the 1930s and 1940s have become very valuable, and are highly sought after. Since their publication was usually not limited to one periodical, these illustrations are sometimes more famous and recognizable than others. At a recent auction of comic and illustration art, the piece that captured the highest price was Joseph Leyendecker's *The Arrow Man,* commissioned by the Arrow Shirt Company, and part of a group of paintings published in the *Saturday Evening Post.* A large oil painting, it sold for over $37,000.

Another very collectible group of illustrations include unpublished works. Original fashion designs, sketched and signed by famous designers, regularly appear on the market, often at a very modest price. Pen and ink or pencil drawings by designers such as Bill Blass, Hubert DeGivenchy, or Oleg Cassini, make an excellent display, and rarely exceed $500 in price. Although their value is most often shaped by the size and elaboration of the drawing and the fame of the designer, a sample of fabric included with the sketch will change its price considerably.

Magazine illustrations have been very popular among collectors and have brought very high prices, but the premier illustrators have worked in books rather than periodicals. Collecting book illustrations can be very difficult, especially since there are thousands of books and artists to learn. An outstanding sourcebook on illustration is Walt and Roger Reed's *The Illustrator in America* (1984), which is still in print and available in libraries.

This book is essential if you are seriously interested in collecting illustration art.

The great majority of American illustration art is contained in books written for children. Many classic novels, such as *Hucklebery Finn* (Charles L. Webster, 1885) and *The Wizard of Oz,* (Chicago: G. M. Hill, 1900), books aimed at both adults and children, have been recognized for the fine quality of their illustrations, but most recent American novels have not included them.

There are dozens of superior children's book illustrators working today, but foremost among them is the legendary Dr. Seuss. Dr. Seuss has written forty-five books, which have sold more than 100 million copies, and he is loved by children (and adults) all over the world. His famous character creations, from the Cat in the Hat to Yertle the Turtle, have in turn initiated everything from toys to animated cartoon specials, making him extremely famous in the process. But more importantly, he has saved thousands of kids from drab children's literature. Says Seuss, "I think I had something to do with kicking Dick and Jane out of the school system. I think I have proved to a number of million kids that reading is not a disagreeable task. And without talking about teaching, I think I have helped kids laugh in schools as well as at home."

Original illustrations from Seuss' work are very difficult to find, but many fine quality illustrations by him, made for collectors, have found their way into the market. Seuss rarely sends out original sketches, and usually answers requests with a signed print of the Cat in the Hat. Responding to one collector's request for an original drawing, Seuss wrote, "If Dr. Seuss drew Cats in the Hats for everyone who asked, his hands would fall off." To another collector who asked for a self-portrait, Seuss responded, saying "I can't draw things the way they are." Yet, when he has made sketches for collectors, they are almost always very handsome works of art and sell for at least $50.

Besides Dr. Seuss, there are a great many other distinguished illustrators of children's books who are currently active. Author and artist Shel Silverstein, who wrote and illustrated *The Giving Tree* (1964) and several other fine volumes, has received wide critical acclaim, as has Richard Scarry, one of today's most respected artists. But the most creative modern illustrator is Maurice Sendak. Sendak has authored and illustrated countless books, including *Where the Wild Things Are* (1963), and his work has been collected in the recent volume, *The Art of Maurice Sendak* (1985). Sendak's work, like that of Dr. Seuss, is also fairly scarce, but his original pencil sketches or drawings are occasionally made available at auction.

Richard Scarry, original drawing of Howly Worm, **$10.**

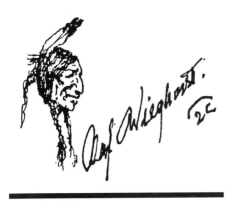

Olaf Weighorst, Indian artist, $55.

Modern illustrators of children's books are relatively easy to keep track of, but once again, *The Illustrator in America* (1984) is a must for identifying artists and gaining an insight into the type of art that is really valuable. In collecting material from the illustrators of older children's books, you will find that there is an enormous amount of collectible material from literally thousands of illustrators. You can see that a good guidebook is absolutely essential to make sense of the field.

The most valuable children's book illustrations are found in books that have become classics. The works of Beatrix Potter, such as *The Tale of Peter Rabbit,* (1903), are filled with wonderful examples of valuable illustration art, as are the *Winnie the Pooh* (E. P. Dutton, 1926), books by A. A. Milne, featuring the work of Ernest Shepard. The works of George Carlson, who illustrated the *Uncle Wiggily* (Platt & Munk, 1920) books by Howard R. Garis, and Garth Williams' illustrations in *Stuart Little* (1945) or *Charlotte's Web* (1952) by E. B. White, or *The Gingerbread Rabbit* (1964) by Randall Jarrell are highly regarded.

Some illustration art from these and other famous illustrators can be purchased at fairly reasonable prices. For example, a pen and ink drawing by A. B. Frost (illustrator of the classic *Uncle Remus* (1895) stories recently sold at auction for the moderate sum of $250. And other bargains may be found if you carefully search out material and try to attend as many auctions as possible.

Even if an illustration was not featured in a classic novel, but is nevertheless part of a famous children's book, it may be very valuable. For instance, many fine illustrators have worked on the popular Golden Books over the years, including Garth Williams, Eloise Wilkin, and Gustaf Tenggren, famous for *The Poky Little Puppy* (1942). A Tenggren watercolor from a Golden Book can cost as much as $1,540, the price realized for a striking example at a Christie's East auction in 1985.

Accomplished American illustrators also have worked outside the realm of children's literature. Sadly, many of today's books for adults forego the use of illustrations, although numerous classics of the past have featured them to great advantage. In attempting to collect the works of these artists it is important to read a little about some of the famous illustrators of the past. Many times, later editions of classic works are illustrated by different artists, and though these originals may be valuable, they will seldom approach the value of the work by the original artist.

Two of the great American illustrators of classic novels are E. W. Kemble, illustrator of Mark Twain's *Huckleberry*

Finn (1885) and W. W. Denslow, who illustrated many of the *Oz* books, by L. Frank Baum. The work of both of these artists is available, although usually in the form of original sketches rather than the actual book illustrations. Denslow made several sketches of *Oz* characters for collectors later in his life, and Kemble, a twenty-three-year-old commercial artist before working on *Huckleberry Finn*, penned several letters filled with fine sketches that have proved popular among both illustration art and manuscript collectors.

Original works by illustrators as respected as Kemble or Denslow have been widely collected, and both of these illustrators have received a great deal of recognition for their work. Unfortunately, many other illustrators of the nineteenth and early twentieth century have escaped great recognition, and much of their work is difficult to locate. Original book illustrations have been donated to museums, or kept by publishers and artists, and are very rare. In chapter 2, we mentioned that animation studios, unaware of the value of original cels and drawings, often discarded originals, or released them to the public. Book publishers and illustrators, however, have always been aware of the great value and importance of original artwork, and only a small fraction of what has been produced has been made available to collectors.

For these reasons, illustration art is available mostly at auction, and is priced substantially. Guernsey's and Christie's are two prestigious auction houses that have featured illustration art, but occasionally the smaller firms

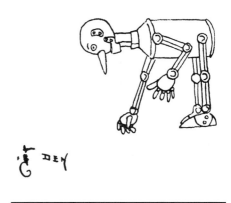

W.W. Denslow, original drawing of the Tin Man, from L. Frank Baum's *The Wizard of Oz*, with his famous seahorse signature, **$350.**

E.W. Kemble, self-portrait, making the drawings for *Huckleberry Finn*, **$500.**

A.B. Frost, original drawing signed, $100.

will have this art for sale. The Society of Illustrators holds an annual Christmas auction of contemporary material that has been donated by its members. To be placed on a mailing list for these auctions, you may write to The Society of Illustrators, 128 East 63rd Street, New York, New York 10021.

Once in a while illustration art may be found in places besides auctions. Private sellers advertise in paper collectible publications, antiques journals, or other magazines devoted to collecting similar material. Sellers of rare books and old magazines are another possible source, although only the largest such dealers usually will handle illustration art. And, of course, very distinguished oil or watercolor works by famous artists may also be found in art galleries.

Original sketches by known illustrators are also sold predominately at auction, but are also available through collectors of autographs and manuscripts, or through some sellers of cartoon art. Several autograph dealers will be listed in the next chapter, and a list of cartoon art dealers may be found in the Appendix. If you are interested in obtaining sketches by contemporary magazine or book illustrators, either may be addressed in care of publishers who are fairly reliable about forwarding requests. The illustrators of children's books are easiest to obtain, followed by magazine illustrators. A few artists of the not-too-distant past may also be reached in care of their magazine or book publishers, although your chances of getting letters to them are not great. Occasionally, a home address for a famous illustrator of the past may be found through one of the address sources listed in the next chapter.

If writing to illustrators in search of sketches does not provide enough for you to do, you might also consider writing to fine artists for a sketch. No artist will make a painting for you, but even a small sketch from a famous artist, such as Salvador Dali, can be worth a great deal. And most artists are happy to oblige if your request is courteous. Norman Rockwell, for instance, loved making sketches for collectors, and several other artists really do appreciate kind letters from admirers.

Collecting illustration art requires both a great deal of hard work and a goodly amount of money. There are problems within the field, including determining value, identifying artists, and finding sources of material at the best possible prices. And since illustration art is so expensive, only the fairly wealthy individual will be able to accumulate a significant collection. Bargains may be found, and original sketches may be solicited from several contemporary artists, but it is advisable to be aware of some of the problems inherent to the field.

However, the work of great illustrators has tremendous historical, cultural, and literary value, and provides a most interesting field of opportunity for all who are interested in original art.

6 | Celebrity Self-Portraits

Celebrity self-portraits are, without a doubt, the most unusual of all cartoon art specialties. Like the field of illustration art, celebrity self-portraits fit loosely within the realm of the cartoon. You may recall, however, that the cartoon had its origins in caricatures of royalty or political leaders. The celebrity self-portrait is most often found in the form of a caricature, and is, therefore, more closely related to the cartoon than originally might seem apparent.

Celebrity self-portraits are generally the most valuable of signed sketches. Original drawings made by famous political leaders, musicians, authors, or even movie stars, may be worth as much as $1,000, or even more, depending upon scarcity and the fame of the celebrity. Artistic quality is only a very small factor in shaping the value of a celebrity drawing. Most celebrities are simply not talented artists, and, if price were determined solely by artistic value, most of the artwork made by celebrities would be valueless. Famous political leaders or film stars, however, are much more recognizable than the average cartoonist, and their artwork often carries a higher price tag.

Three sketches made by Ronald Reagan, **$1,000.**

One of the problems involved in collecting celebrity self-portraits is that few dealers of comic, animation, or even illustration art handle them. They are available primarily through dealers of autographs, manuscripts, or historical documents, and are sometimes difficult to locate even through these sources. The majority of famous historical figures or contemporary personalities have never made drawings of themselves and, consequently, self-portraits are among the rarest forms of autographs.

If you would like to collect self-portraits or other celebrity drawings, you should become acquainted with the hobby of autograph collecting. Autograph collecting, as a hobby, is much more organized than the field of cartoon art, but it is also more complex. There are more problems involving authenticity and finding reputable sellers who are part of the autograph hobby than in cartoon art collecting. Yet, if you gain an understanding of some of the basics of autograph collecting, the hobby's complexities will not affect you to a great degree.

Unlike the cartoon art field, there are several clubs or organizations devoted to the autograph hobby. However, only one organization is really worth joining if your main interest is self-portraits of celebrities. The other organizations are for movie star autograph collectors, or manuscript buyers, and do not provide a good general overview of the field. The Universal Autograph Collector's Club, Albert W. Witnnebert, 2621 S.W. 66th Terrace, Miramar, Florida 33023 is not only the best autograph club, it is also the largest worldwide. Each issue of the club's journal, *The Pen & Quill*, provides addresses of famous personalities in all fields, collecting tips, and information about autograph auctions. In addition, once you are listed in *The Pen & Quill* as a club member, dozens of autograph dealers will add your name to their mailing lists, and you can gain valuable information about how autographs are priced, and also, of course, have the opportunity to purchase autographs or celebrity artwork. Annual membership dues for the club are currently $15 per year.

Several autograph publications and books are also available that provide helpful information about the hobby. The books of noted collector Charles Hamilton are excellent source books for illustrations of autographs and his *The Signature of America* (1979) also includes many self-portraits and other artwork by celebrities. Although it is currently out-of-print, it may be found in your local library. For an introduction to the hobby, my own *A Collector's Guide to Autographs* (1986) should prove informative. The best autograph publication providing balanced coverage of all fields and specialties is *The Autograph Collector's Magazine,* $12 yearly, from P.O. Box 55328, Stockton, California 95205, with two hundred addresses of famous personalities in each issue. It is also a good idea to join the Universal Autograph Collector's Club and to write to several autograph dealers and ask to be placed on their mailing list. Since you are a collector of self-portraits, rather than autographs, you should also mention this to the dealer in your letter. The dealers will more than likely inform you whether or not they feature such material in their catalogs. The Universal Autograph Collector's Club has published a directory listing seventy-one autograph dealers, and is available from the club for $6.50 postpaid. This list will help you contact sellers of celebrity self-portaits, as well as other types of cartoon art.

Quite a few autograph dealers regularly sell celebrity self-portraits, or other kinds of cartoon art in their catalogs. Robert Le Gresley Autographs, P.O. Box 1199, Lawrence, Kansas 66004, has offered self-portraits, original strips, original sketches, illustration art, and signed letters from famous cartoonists. His catalogs are free upon request.

Paul Hartunian Autographs, 47 Portland Place, Montclair, New Jersey 07042, sponsors mail auction and autograph sales. He has featured original in-person sketches of cartoonists on album leaves, and occasionally includes self-portraits in his lists. Catalogs are free upon request.

Jeanne Hoyt Autographs, P.O. Box 1517, Rohnert Park, California 94928, offers autographs of film stars, sports stars and literary personalities. Once in a while a self-portrait appears for sale in a catalog. In addition, Hoyt usually offers original magazine cartoons in her lists, which are free upon request.

Monroe Mendoza, 102-10 66th Road, Forest Hills, New York 11375, is an outstanding source of inexpensive autographed material. Cartoon art is a part of nearly every listing. Catalogs are free upon request.

The autograph dealers who feature historical documents, and letters signed by famous historical personalities are less likely to handle cartoon art. Occasionally, self-portraits are made available to prospective buyers, however. These dealers include The Scriptorium, 427 North Canon Drive, Beverly Hills, California 90210, and Herman M. Darvick Autographs, P.O.

George Gershwin, **\$400.**

Emmett Kelly, **\$60.**

Box 467, Rockville Centre, New York 11571.

If you are seriously interested in celebrity art, and would like to pursue it through dealers of autographs, it is wise to write to as many dealers as possible in order to obtain their catalogs. The Universal Autograph Collector's Club dealer's guide is an essential tool, and with it you can solicit enough listings to acquire a working knowledge of prices.

Author Georges Simenon, $70.

Even these dealers may not have self-portraits for sale on a regular basis, so you might try the direct approach and send a well-phrased letter to the celebrity's home. Although requests may be sent to an office or agency address, the home address of a celebrity provides you with the best chance of getting the request into the celebrity's hands. Home addresses are not as hard to find as might be expected, and are available for personalities in a wide variety of fields. *The Autograph Collector's Magazine,* and the Universal Autograph Collector's Club's *The Pen & Quill* provide addresses in each issue, but there are also a wide variety of home address lists that are for sale.

The best source of movie star or popular musician addresses is Roger and Karen Christensen's *The Ultimate Movie, TV and Rock Directory.* The last edition (1985) is currently out-of-print, but a new edition should be out shortly. To receive more information about this publication, write to 6065 Mission Gorge Road, Suite 217, San Diego, California 92120.

Another publication, which is almost entirely composed of addresses, is *Autograph Collector,* 1111 Clairmont J-1, Decatur, Georgia 30030. This jour-

nal regularly updates many celebrity addresses and is a trusted source of accurate information. Send a self-addressed, stamped envelope with your request for more information.

A.C.S., 1765 N. Highland Avenue #434, Hollywood, California 90028, is a firm that sells celebrity addresses for 50 cents each. A listing of available addresses is an additional $2.00. A.C.S. is more expensive than the average source, but since they feature accurate and up-to-the-minute information, it may be a good idea to consider patronizing them.

Jim Weaver, 405 Dunbar Drive, Pittsburgh, Pennsylvania 15235, features address lists including many different personalities, but mainly film stars or musicians. Weaver's lists are fairly inexpensive; send a self-addressed, stamped envelope with your request for more information.

Home or good office addresses for famous personalities may also be found in books available at the library, such as *Who's Who in America, The International Who's Who, Who's Who in American Politics,* and *Current Biography.* If the celebrity hasn't reached the level of fame where they are besieged with fan mail, addresses published in these sources are often good enough to bring responses.

When you are writing to a celebrity, always make sure that your letter is polite and respectful, and that you enclose a self-addressed, stamped envelope. Be aware also, that most celebrities will *not* make a self-portrait for you even if your letter requesting one is especially nice. Many celebrities simply have no desire to make drawings of themselves for others, possibly because they may not consider themselves accomplished artists, or they just may be too modest. Whatever the reason, don't always expect to receive one. Celebrities who refuse to make self-portraits might, however, make another type of drawing for you if your request is appealing, and these may be equally valuable. One collector, for instance, had the idea of asking every celebrity to sketch an elephant, and received many interesting replies. And even if you manage to obtain only the celebrity's autograph, you will have acquired something worthwhile.

The foremost difficulty involved in collecting autographs is authenticating the autograph you have received through the mail (or purchased from a dealer). Thankfully, this is not a major problem in collecting cartoon art, or even celebrity self-portraits. A secretary or forger may sign a celebrity's name for them, but they will hardly ever make a self-portrait of the celebrity. The possibility of making too many mistakes will discourage a forger, while a secretary may not feel authorized to make a drawing of his/her boss. In either case, you can take heart in the fact that almost all celebrity drawings are authentic and original. There are exceptions to this, of course (such as the recent forgeries of some of John Lennon's artwork), but they will seldom affect your enjoyment of the hobby.

Whether you buy celebrity art from a dealer, or try obtaining it yourself by mail, it is advisable to concentrate your collection on one or a few distinct groups of celebrities. You may wish to specialize in collecting artwork from famous historical personalities—U.S. presidents, royalty, classical musicians of the past, or literary figures of the

Sinclair Lewis, **$175.**

Allen Ginsberg, **$20.**

137

John Lennon, signature incorporating a small sketch of himself, **$125.**

past. Or, you might want to consider collecting more contemporary personalities. But, if you decide to specialize in one or a few areas, you will be able to assemble a better collection, and one that is more valuable as well. Each area of specialization requires different collecting skills, and learning about each field takes time. In collecting literary personalities you have to do a little research on authors of the past and find out the comparative values of their artwork or autographs. If you approach the hobby from an investment standpoint, this knowledge is essential in order to make the best investments.

Many historical personalities have been famous for their self-portraits. The artwork of these celebrities, such as classical musicians or authors, often appears on the market in the form of illustrated letters or small sketches. The work of political or military leaders is less common, but is available on occasion. President Theodore Roosevelt wrote letters to his children and often illustrated them with sketches.

Musicians and opera stars often are fine artists and caricaturists, and much of their material is readily available. Enrico Caruso's self-portraits are plentiful as are sketches of other famous musical personalities of his day. Caruso was a fine artist, and his original artwork makes an outstanding display. The great composer George Gershwin was also known for his drawings of himself and his musical circle, and his artwork showed a surprising degree of talent.

Authors, poets, and other literary figures of the past are outstanding sources of original drawings, as many of their letters or manuscript pages contain sketches or self-portraits. Material on literary personalities is also very plentiful, although it is very expensive. Among great writers, a few stand out as fine artists, including O. Henry and William Faulkner. Faulkner's illustrations, appearing in his early novels, are highly prized, and the work of O. Henry, known for his brilliant sketches of friends and acquaintances, is both valuable and highly unusual. Other famous novelists, notably Mark Twain and Sinclair Lewis, have been considerably less talented. Twain's drawings are particularly awful, and in his day, his artwork was parodied by other artists, such as Thomas Nast. Many of the sketches of F. Scott Fitzgerald also survive today, and, though highly entertaining, they are nevertheless usually crude and amateurish, perhaps because many were made while he was drunk.

Contemporary authors and poets are sometimes persuaded to make self-portraits or other drawings, and the work of authors Allen Ginsberg, Erica Jong, or Laurence Ferlinghetti has occasionally appeared on the market. An excellent book containing self-portraits of contemporary authors is Burt Britton's *Self-Portrait: Book People Picture Themselves* (1976) published by Random House, and available in larger libraries.

Film and television stars are another excellent source of original art. Many stars incorporate small sketches and self-portraits into their signatures, and some may also be persuaded to create more elaborate works of art. In the early days of Hollywood, dozens of great stars took the time to make sketches in autograph albums; this material frequently appears for sale today. Charlie Chaplin and Ben Turpin were both known for their excellent additions to these albums, and their sketches are now worth upwards of $100 each. Harpo Marx drew hilarious sketches on dozens of old album pages. Today, movie star self-portraits are far less common on album leaves,

Enrico Caruso, **$400.**

139

W.C. Fields, **$200.**

as most of today's stars, when approached in person, rarely take the time even to sign their names. Collecting through the mail is much more practical, and for the price of postage, self-portraits of dozens of famous stars may be added to your collection.

Collecting self-portraits from contemporary personalities can be a great deal more enjoyable if you try to collect a wide variety of personalities from many different fields. Specialization is important for investment purposes, as there are many intricacies present in each of the hobby's specialties, but for pure enjoyment or show purposes, a diverse collection is highly recommended. To achieve this collection, you must use your imagination. Besides collecting literary personalities or film stars, why not try collecting self-portraits or artwork from sports stars, scientists, astronauts, Supreme Court justices, famous women, military leaders, Nobel prize winners, or cabinet members, to name just a few of the endless possibilities.

Collecting celebrity self-portraits may even lead you into the world of collecting celebrity paintings. Dozens of famous names, both past and present, have been noted for their paintings, including Adolf Hitler, Dwight Eisenhower, Sir Winston Churchill, and several movie and musical stars. These paintings are often expensive due to the great fame of the artists, but they also can make excellent investment purchases.

If it goes
up it goes down
for you it was uh
So good!

Zero Mostel

Zero Mostel, **$50.**

William Powell, sketch of himself in character as The Thin Man, **$45.**

Edgar Bergen, two sketches of his characters, including Mortimer Snerd, **$50.**

Arthur Lake, star of many "Blondie" films, self-portrait, **$15.**

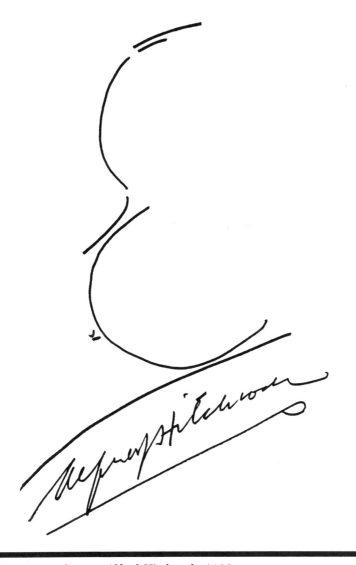

Famed motion picture director Alfred Hitchcock, **$100.**

Comedienne Phyllis Diller, **$5.**

Charlie Chaplin, symbolic self-portrait, **$175.**

Leonard Kibrick, portrait of himself as a child when he appeared in Hal Roach's *Our Gang* (or *Little Rascals*) comedies, **$15.**

We have noted several differences between celebrity art and comic, animation, or illustration art, in this chapter. One that merits further exploration is the difference in the way value is determined. Comic or animation art value is based primarily on the fame of the character, the quality of the art, or its role in a production process. The fame of the artist is important, but not as essential as the other factors. The name of the artist is most important in the field of celebrity art. The price of celebrity art is shaped by supply and demand, but people collect celebrity drawings for a different reason than they would collect comic or animation art. The quality of the drawing is certainly a factor in pricing celebrity art, but is of lesser significance than the popularity and appeal of the artist or the scarcity of the artist's signature or artwork. In other words, the art of Mark Twain can be very valuable even though it is of very poor quality. It is much more valuable than the artwork of any modern cartoonist, even though the cartoonist may be a brilliant artist. The value of celebrity art, then, is related to the value of the celebrity's signature. Price is determined by the intensity of people's preferences for the signature (demand) and the rarity of the signature (supply). The quality of the artwork only serves to add to the quality of the piece and increase its price.

Silent comedian Ben Turpin, $85.

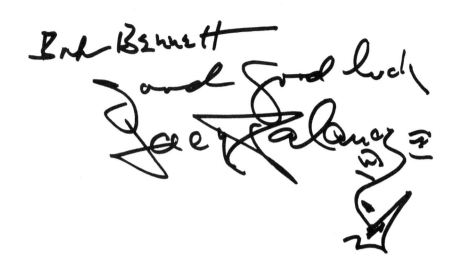

Jack Palance, signature incorporating a small sketch, **$5.**

Celebrity self-portraits, although not traditionally related to cartoon art, may offer you the chance to truly broaden and improve your cartoon art collection. Imagine a collection based not only upon sketches, strips, or cels featuring famous characters, but also upon original drawings of famous persons as well. Collecting the celebrity self-portrait may indeed be difficult for you, especially if you are accustomed to the field of cartoon art, and do not wish to become acquainted with the field of autograph collecting. Yet, if you find it more enjoyable to write to famous personalities, rather than cartoonists, or if you are more interested in history, science, or music than cartoons, then this field may be for you. It certainly offers almost limitless possibilities for interest, enjoyment, and appreciation.

Appendix

Major Comic Strip Syndicators

King Features Syndicate
235 E. 45th Street
New York, NY 10017

News America Syndicate
1703 Kaiser Avenue
Irvine, CA 92714

Newspaper Enterprise Association
200 Park Avenue
New York, NY 10166

Tribune Media Services
64 E. Concord Street
Orlando, FL 32801

United Feature Syndicate
200 Park Avenue
New York, NY 10166

Universal Press Syndicate
4900 Main Street, 9th Floor
Kansas City, MO 62114

Washington Post Writers Group
1150 15th Street, N.W.
Washington, DC 20071

Publications

The Big Reel
Route #3, Box 239-A
Madison, NC 27025

Comic Book Price Guide
By R.M. Overstreet.
Available in bookstores

Comics Buyer's Guide
700 E. State Street
Iola, WI 54990

Comics Journal
4359 Cornell
Agoura, CA 91301

Movie Collector's World
P.O. Box 309
Fraser, MI 48026

Nemo Magazine
4359 Cornell
Agoura, CA 91301

Paper Collector's Marketplace
700 E. State Street
Iola, WI 54990

Sellers of Cartoon Art

Berry Auction Company
8380 Santa Monica Blvd.
Los Angeles, CA 90069

Cartoon Museum
4300 S. Semoran Blvd. #409
Orlando, FL 32822

Christie's East
219 E. 67th Street
New York, NY 10021

Cohasco, Inc.
Postal 821
Yonkers, NY 10702

Collectable Books
2217 Defense Hwy.
Crofton, MD 21114

Comic Carnival
408 Bickmore Road
Wallingford, PA 19086

Comic Castle
107 W. Amerige
Fullerton, CA 92632

Comic Gallery
4224 Balboa Ave.
San Diego, CA 92117

Comics Paradise Gallery
P.O. Box 1540
Studio City, CA 91604

Robert A. LeGresley
P.O. Box 1199
Lawrence, KS 66004

Bibliography

Adamson, Joe. *Tex Avery: King of Cartoons.* New York: Popular Library, 1975.

Bennett, Bob. *A Collector's Guide to Autographs with Prices.* Lombard, Ill.: Wallace-Homestead, 1986.

Hamilton, Charles. *The Signature of America:* New York: Harper and Row, 1979.

Horn, Maurice. *The World Encyclopedia of Comics.* New York: Chelsea House, 1976.

Maltin, Leonard. *Of Mice and Magic: A History of American Animated Cartoons.* New York: McGraw Hill, 1980.

Index

About the Author

Bob Bennett's interest in collecting animated cartoons and the comics began as an offshoot of his other hobby, autograph collecting.

Born in Rutland, Vermont, in 1963, and raised in Vermont and New Jersey, Bennett became a dedicated autograph collector when he joined the Universal Autograph Collector's Club in 1978. He completed his first book, *A Collector's Guide to Autographs,* in 1986, and is currently a director of the Universal Autograph Collector's Club.

Bennett has authored many articles in his magazine, *Newsreel,* which he began in 1982. He has also written for several other publications, including *Movie Collector's World, The Pen and Quill, Hollywood Tribute, Libertarian Party News,* and *The Burlington Free Press,* on a wide variety of topics, from movies to politics. In addition, he has been a two-time candidate for the Vermont legislature.

Bennett, a 1985 graduate of the University of Vermont with a major in Political Science, is now a student at Albany Law School, Albany, New York.